Using HUMOR for Effective Business Speaking

GENE PERRET

Foreword by Og Mandino

 Sterling Publishing Co., Inc.   New York

Library of Congress Cataloging-in-Publication Data

Perret, Gene.
    Using humor for effective business speaking / by Gene Perret ;
foreword by Og Mandino.
        p.   cm.
    Includes index.
    ISBN 0-8069-6878-8
    1. Public speaking.   2. Wit and humor.   3. Business communication.
I. Title.
PN4193.B8P47   1989
808.5'1—dc19   88-34669
                                                                                    CIP

Copyright © 1989 by Gene Perret
Published by Sterling Publishing Co., Inc.
Two Park Avenue, New York, N.Y. 10016
Distributed in Canada by Oak Tree Press Ltd.
℅ Canadian Manda Group, P.O. Box 920, Station U
Toronto, Ontario, Canada M8Z 5P9
Distributed in Great Britain and Europe by Cassell PLC
Artillery House, Artillery Row, London SW1P 1RT, England
Distributed in Australia by Capricorn Ltd.
P.O. Box 665, Lane Cove, NSW 2066
Manufactured in the United States of America

To
Mary, Phil,
Joe, and Fran

"We need humor as much as we need any other kind of sustenance in our daily lives."

David Graves

Contents

FOREWORD   9

Part I—The Business of Humor in Business   11
  1   The Power of Humor   13
  2   What Humor Does for the Speaker   19
  3   The Dignity of Humor   35
  4   Overcoming the Fear of Humor   43
  5   Humor and the Business Executive   51
  6   Humor Is Not Necessarily Jokes   61
  7   But I'm Not a Funny Person   71

Part II—Creating Your Humor   81
  8   Okay—How Do I Go About Giving
      Humor a Try?   83
  9   How Much Humor Should I Use?   93
  10 Where Do the Jokes Go?   99
  11 Where Do I Get Good Material?   109
  12 How Do I Make the Humor Pertinent?   121
  13 Can I Really Write My Own?   127
  14 Put Yourself Into Your Humor   147
  15 Some Humor Exercises: (Just to
      Prove You Can Do It)   159

Part III—Delivering Your Humor   171
  16 Tips on Delivering Humor   173
  17 How Do I Know the Jokes Will Work?   185
  18 How Do I Avoid Offending Anyone?   197

19 Pitfalls That Take the Fun Out
    of Humor   *209*
20 Humor in the Workplace   *217*

ABOUT THE AUTHOR   *220*

INDEX   *221*

Foreword

Gene Perret writes humor, teaches humor, and he lives humor. He writes it because that's how he earns his living. He teaches it because it's fun. He lives it because he believes in it.

The first time I heard Gene speak was about ten years ago. He was giving a seminar on humor to an audience of professional speakers. He claimed in his opening that he didn't have a momentous message for any of us. Marketing wasn't his forte. He couldn't teach us how to get more bookings. Time management confused him, and his desk and office were hardly fitting samples of organization.

He said, "I told my wife I'm going to travel some distance, I'm going to work very hard, and no one's going to learn anything. I don't know if I can do it. She said, 'Sure you can, Gene. Just remember our honeymoon.'"

Here was a respected comedy writer inviting us to a laugh at his wife's friendly put-down. Here was a humorist using humor to teach us how to use humor effectively.

We laughed and we listened. We learned that a clever use of humor can capture and captivate an audience. We were all speakers; we all had a message. But a message is useless unless we, the speakers, get people to listen and to remember. That was Gene's message that day.

That's also the point of this very special book. In these pages Gene is reminding all of us that if we have something worth saying, it should be worth listening to, also. Humor is one of the tools that can grab and hold an audience's attention.

Perret is worth listening to. When he talks about comedy, the best in the world listen. Bob Hope has been performing comedy for over 60 years, yet he says, "When I need some extra special material I call on Gene. He's my trouble shooter."

You'll find him worth listening to, also, because he practices what he preaches. His sense of humor translates to the written page. The lessons are worthwhile, the substance is there, but it's delivered in an entertaining, anecdotal style. Again, it's the humorist using humor to teach humor.

I've been a friend of Gene Perret's since we first met after that speaker's seminar. We've shared the platform a few times, and we've exchanged speaker's and writer's war stories many evenings. Gene lives what he preaches. Humor is not only part of his life; it's his way of life.

His writing is delightful; his speaking is entertaining; most importantly, he's fun to be with.

You'll enjoy spending time with him in the pages of this book, and you'll learn much about communicating with humor.

Here's one of his anecdotes that's not in this book, but it tells you how Gene feels about humor. It's a story Gene is very proud of, but only shares with friends. I'm sharing it with you.

Gene had been asked by Bob Hope to write some lyrics for a song. He didn't feel that was his strongest writing skill, but he finished the assignment. Gene says:

"When I handed Bob Hope the pages, he asked, 'Is it brilliant?' I said, 'Bob, if I could write brilliant song lyrics, would I still be writing comedy?' Hope looked me in the eye and said, 'Yeah, you would, Gene. You would.'"

Bob Hope was right. Gene's still writing comedy, still speaking with humor, and still teaching humor. I'm glad.

Og Mandino
Author/Lecturer
September, 1988

PART I

The Business of Humor in Business

"One horselaugh is worth ten thousand syllogisms. It is not only more effective; it is vastly more intelligent."

H. L. Mencken

CHAPTER ONE

The Power of Humor

There is a speech that is delivered every single day of the year. In fact, it's delivered thousands of times daily. It's an important speech, yet hardly anyone listens to it. It's the safety instructions that flight attendants must deliver before each flight.

Some of us don't listen because we don't want to admit that something might go wrong with this flight. Let other people on other flights listen—the flights that might have problems. Some of us seasoned travellers are too arrogant to listen. We know all there is to know about planes and exits and what to do and when to do it. When this discourse begins, we smugly snap open our attache cases, take out yellow pads and begin our personal work. We want the other passengers to know that our business is more important than any life-saving procedures might be.

Others don't listen because they're too busy trying to stuff their sixth carry-on bag into the overhead compartment—on top of my neatly folded suit jacket.

These safety instructions are probably the most universally ignored lecture in history.

I was on a flight recently, though, where everyone listened and heard the instructions. The flight attendant introduced herself and her assistants over the intercom. Newspapers rattled, briefcases popped open, bags were pounded into non-existent spaces in already filled overhead compartments. Not a head snapped forward in attention.

"There may be 50 ways to leave your lover," the attendant said, "but there are only five ways to leave this airplane." There were a few chuckles and people glanced around from behind the open lids of the briefcases. We were confused. Had we boarded a plane or a nightclub? We listened to make sure.

The attendant continued. She was determined to have us know just where the exits were. "Even if you know where these exits are, please turn around and locate the one nearest you. We noticed when you boarded that there are some pretty good-looking men and women on this flight—you know who you are. We think the people sitting behind you deserve to get a look at you, too." Everyone proudly turned around and chuckled.

We were all caught up in her monologue now and wanted to hear more.

"In preparation for take-off," she said, "please return your seat backs to their full upright, locked, and most uncomfortable position. Later you may lean back and break the knees of the passenger behind you."

She was getting solid laughs now, and people who normally travel coast to coast without communicating with any person or thing besides their pocket calculator, were smiling, nodding, and actually talking to one another.

The flight attendant went on to explain where our oxygen masks would come from and how we were to operate them. She told us that we could fasten them exactly the way the flight attendants were now demonstrating, "Except," she added, "when you put yours on, you're allowed to muss your hair."

"Those of you travelling with small children, or just people acting like small children, should put your masks on first."

This young lady forced us to listen to a message that we didn't want to hear. She had conquered "white knucklers" and seasoned travelers. She overpowered us with humor.

I thought there were tremendous lessons in this demonstration. First of all, she did get us to listen. She harnessed a reluctant audience. Her message was a potentially life-saving one. She got us to hear it. Second, she livened up her own act. Probably, she was bored giving this same talk over and over again, but with these new twists, she added a little gusto. She seemed to relish the laughter, and in fact, when she finished, the applause. Third, she created a more pleasant atmosphere. People were laughing, kidding with one another and enjoying the safety instructions.

It carried over into the flight. We were all more pleasant than usual with the flight attendants and with each other.

That's the power of humor that business people shouldn't overlook. Wouldn't all of us love to be able to get reluctant customers or employees to listen to our important messages? Wouldn't we pay gladly to have them pay attention when they don't want to? Wouldn't we offer almost anything to have them listen and hear our side of a story when they've already made up their minds—knowing they have nothing to learn from us? This young lady did it; why can't we in business do it?

Wouldn't we love to enjoy our tasks as much as this airline employee enjoyed hers? Wouldn't it be nice to get the reception she got? They actually applauded safety instructions.

Wouldn't we be more valuable if we could create the same kind of climate in the office that this woman created on the plane? It was a long flight and her talk lasted only a few minutes, but what an impact those few minutes had. She improved morale on that aircraft, and it endured.

Let's look at another example. In this illustration, there was some money on the line—quite a bit of money. It was a court case that involved a Mississippi river barge that accidentally rammed and damaged a newly built railroad bridge over the river. The railroad was suing for recovery.

The barge owner disputed the railroad's right to interfere with navigation. Because the case had such far-reaching consequences, the railroads loaded the courtroom with their best and highest paid attorneys.

The case was complicated, long, and tedious. The railroad lawyers presented logical evidence that impressed the jurors. The barge owner retained a single lawyer. In his closing argument he admitted to the jury, "My learned opponents have presented an impressive case. There is no question that they have their facts absolutely right. But they have drawn completely wrong conclusions."

The jurors laughed heartily. Then they adjourned and returned quickly with a verdict in favor of the barge owner.

What happened? The losing attorneys wanted to know, too. They asked the country lawyer. His name was Abraham Lincoln.

As the story goes, Lincoln confessed that he ran into the jurors at lunch that afternoon and told them a tale about a farmer whose young son came rushing up to him. "Pa," the boy said, "come quick. Sis and the hired hand are up in the hayloft. She's got her skirt hiked up and he's got his overalls down. If you don't come quick, Pa, I think they might pee all over our hay." "Son," the farmer said, "you've got your facts right, but you've drawn a completely wrong conclusion."

Probably all of us saw, heard, or at least read about another example of the power of humor. Some feel it may have gotten a man re-elected to the Presidency of the United States.

When Ronald Reagan campaigned for re-election, age was quite a concern among the voters. He would have been, at the end of his second term, the oldest President ever to hold the office. His first debate with Walter Mondale didn't help him. Most analysts thought he did badly. He looked tired; he looked old.

Mondale couldn't attack too viciously, because he didn't want to appear to be the heavy who was ousting a man from his post because of age. He didn't really have to attack too strenuously anyway. Reagan's tired, confused appearance was more telling than any remarks Mondale could have made.

The pressure was on Reagan to bounce back in the second presidential debate. He had to respond to the unasked age question. He got his opportunity.

One of the questioners said, "Mr. President, you already are the oldest President in history, and some of your staff say you were tired after your most recent encounter with Mr. Mondale. I recall that President Kennedy had to go for days on end with very little sleep during the Cuban missile crisis. Is there any doubt in your mind that you would be able to function in such circumstances?"

The journalist was really asking, "Are you too old to be President?"

Reagan said, "I want you to know that I will not make age an issue in this campaign. I am not going to exploit, for political purposes, my opponent's youth and inexperience."

Even Mondale laughed. The audience laughed and applauded. The line was quoted on the front pages of most newspapers the next day as the turning point in the debates.

Humor can have that kind of power.

Understand, though, that humor isn't always the dramatic, quotable line that makes the morning paper and alters history. If it does, and it can, fine. But it's still a powerful everyday tool even if you don't have professional writers turning out your quips. A good sense of humor—and a wise use of humor—is mostly an attitude. It's a commonsense way of looking at yourself and the world around you.

One last caution—this is a book about humor and how it can be an executive tool. The examples I use are naturally examples of humor. And it doesn't take much. Lincoln, Reagan, and the other people mentioned in these pages, didn't go around doing jokes during the entire day. These short, isolated examples show not only how well and how wisely they used humor but also how sparingly.

Noel Coward said, "Wit ought to be a glorious treat, like caviar; never spread it around like marmalade."

These pages don't want to turn promising executives and competent business speakers into comedy club performers. You're not on the podium to get laughs, applause, and critical reviews; you're there to make a point.

Humor, though, can be a powerful ally in getting your message across. It's an ally that many in the business world neglect or ignore. It has power and it should be used.

Where does this power come from? What can humor do for a speaker and how does it do it? Let's take a look.

CHAPTER TWO

What Humor Does for the Speaker

The speaker seems to have all of the advantages in a meeting room. All the chairs are aimed in his or her direction. A lectern is provided for notes. Perhaps a podium even elevates the speaker a foot or so above the audience. No one else has a microphone. Yet the speaker has one drawback—he or she is horribly outnumbered.

Most talks begin as an adversary confrontation. That's not to say that each speaker walks into an auditorium and greets a lynch mob, but there is a dash of suspicion in most crowds. And a touch of resentment. The audience asks itself, "Who are you to presume to teach me anything?" "How come you're up there in the spotlight and I'm down here in the cheap seats?"

Of course, with well-known performers, that suspicion might not exist. The listeners know them and their credentials. They've accepted their expertise. But if you're an ordinary business speaker, you may still have to prove yourself. You have to win the audience to your side. You may not always convert them to your point of view, but you should at least convince them that you have the right to offer them a point of view.

Humor can help accomplish this conversion in several ways.

1. Humor generates respect: I've made a few military trips into war zones with the Bob Hope Show. One incident that happened at sea off the coast of Beirut, Lebanon, illustrates how respect affects the power of a speaker. We had just finished a show and our cast and crew were milling about waiting for a helicopter to carry us back to our home ship, the *USS Guam*. Our work was done for the day, so this was R & R—social time, party time—for us. We were guests of the military, but none of the military discipline had rubbed off on us.

The officers were trying to maintain some order so that when our helicopters landed on deck, we could quickly load and evacuate. Our crew was competent and knew what they were doing, but they didn't line up two-by-two in alphabetical order. They relaxed and chatted until a job had to be done; then they did it quickly and efficiently.

We had one "weekend soldier" who was assigned to this trip with us. He worked at NBC and was also an officer in the Marine Reserves, so he seemed a perfect liaison officer to accompany us. He wasn't.

Carried away with the bars he had earned during his weekend tours of duty, he appointed himself the reformer who would bring order out of our unregulated chaos. He jumped up on some loading crates. His spit-polished jumping boots reflected the sun; his neatly pressed camouflaged fatigues screamed military authority. He barked in his fiercest marine drill instructor voice, "I want the following people to report to me front and center on the double . . . ." Then he yelled out the names of a few of our crew members.

It was such a jarring display that our chatting ceased. Everyone turned and looked and listened—for just a second. Then seeing who it was, we turned back to our chatter.

He grew red-faced barking orders, but no line of personnel ever formed in front of his make-shift podium. We certainly heard him. He bellowed so loudly that the Shiites in the Druze Mountains probably heard him. But no one listened.

Then choppers approached the ship. Our staging supervisor issued a few quiet orders and cameramen, electricians, sound men, all moved with orderly precision. We loaded our gear and personnel, lifted off, and flew back to our ship. We listened to one of the men because we respected him and ignored the other.

Of course, we knew both people. We had been living with them and working with them for several days. They had established their credentials—good and bad. A speaker must establish that respect within the first few minutes of meeting the audience.

Authority doesn't do it. The first gentleman had the military demeanor and the rank. It meant nothing. Authority, in fact, may be a hindrance. So you're the boss. That just means that you want something from this crowd. Sure you want us to work harder, improve your standing with your superiors, and perhaps get you promoted.

Besides, your audience may be convinced that management is the least competent part of the work unit. Don't many executives rise to their level of incompetency? Aren't the people who really know what should be done working in the mail room or as janitors?

That's how your audience might think.

The TV show M*A*S*H used to highlight this attitude each week. Every officer above the rank of the stars, except for Colonel Potter, who was somehow exempt, was an imbecile. So were the people in Washington. Every person of any authority was an idiot. It's a false notion, but a notion that exists. It's a notion that a speaker, as an authority figure, must overcome.

Humor is an excellent way of gaining respect. You may not have a problem with this. Your work record and the business decisions you've made may already have established you as a person who should be listened to. That's great. However, any time you face a new, unfamiliar audience, you have to overcome that sliver of doubt. Humor can help you do it.

Humor that encapsulates the situation and defines it is the best type for earning that respect. It tells your audience quickly and concisely, "I know what the situation is, and I know you know what the situation is. Now I have something to say that's worth listening to."

2. Humor gets the listeners' attention: I've heard some people say, "My message is too important to include humor." Wasn't Ronald Reagan's message important? He wanted to become President again and had invested millions of dollars in the effort. Wasn't Lincoln's message critical? He needed to win an important and potentially costly case for his client.

If you feel your message is truly important, you want to have it heard. Why not use every method available to make sure people get it?

I like the example of the woman who resorted to whimsy to get a reply from her grandchildren at college. The parents complained that the youngsters never wrote. Grandmom said she'd send a letter and get a reply within a week. She did. She received a pleasant page of happy chatter from the campus, ending with, "And Grandmom, you did mention that you were enclosing a check, but there was none in the letter."

People love to be entertained; they love to laugh. Have you noticed at trade shows and conventions how the booths that draw the biggest crowds offer some sort of gimmick—a magician, a game, or something like that? Fun attracts people.

At parties, people glance with envy at the crowd in the corner who are laughing and enjoying an entertaining conversation.

The friends you value most, on reflection, are often the ones that you have the most fun with.

It's human nature; we all love a good time.

Sometimes at seminars or conventions I will speak at concurrent sessions. I'll be speaking in banquet room A, while banquet room B hosts a seminar on "Zero Based Budgeting," and room C has a lecture on "Personnel Problems of the '80s." I always instruct my audience: "Laugh loud and hard even if you don't like some of the jokes. Let's make the people in the other rooms think *they* picked the wrong session to attend."

Every speaker should be aware, too, that just because people are in the room, staring up at you, with notebooks open on their laps and pens poised, that doesn't mean they're paying attention. Minds can wander easily and they leave no tracks. Those bright blue eyes in the third row that are staring up as you speak may be wondering what dress to wear to the awards banquet tonight. The guy in the fourth row may be looking at the lady in the third row and wondering if he should ask her to dance after the awards banquet no matter what dress she wears.

I remember the ultimate in inattention once when I was working on a story conference for the television show, *Three's Company.* As producer, I had brought a difficult story problem to two of the executive producers for their solution. They pondered for a while, then one of the execs popped up enthusiastically with a possible answer. He said, "How about this idea?" Then he acted out the entire scene, complete with business, props, and pratfalls. It took him about four minutes and considerable energy to get his idea across. Finally, he turned to his partner and said, "So . . . what do you think?" His partner said, "I'm sorry, Bernie. I wasn't listening."

When you include some light-hearted humor and entertainment in your talk, listeners perk up. They table their daydreams about this afternoon's golf-tourney or tonight's cocktail party in favor of a little fun right here and now.

I recently heard a speaker in California who lectured on the same day that a mild earthquake shook the area. She mentioned that there is a theory that our animals, if watched closely, can give us hints about when a tremor is due. She said, "If I had paid attention to my pets I would have known an earthquake was coming. They gave me a clue. Last night the two dogs took the family car and drove to Arizona."

Her audience listened pretty well.

3. Humor holds their attention: None of us are creatures who are designed to stay on one subject too long. We tire of it; we look for variety, diversions. While you're speaking about business trends and expectations, your audience may be wondering where you bought that tie and if it's really silk.

Listening to a talk, even a beneficial one, is work. The mind of the listener has to cooperate with the speaker. It has to absorb, analyze, and judge the material. It's almost like studying. The audience eventually hits a saturation point. When that happens, they need a recess.

That's the value of a short coffee break at work. It's why you forget about the problems at the office and take in a movie once in a while. It's why a boxer needs a one-minute rest between rounds. It's a chance to recover and regroup.

A speech may be momentous, but it's also exhausting. To keep an audience attentive, you have to give them a little ice-pack on the back of the neck between rounds. You need to offer a little refreshment so they can maintain their stamina.

You don't need much. Just a little break—maybe a funny quote, or a one-liner. An anecdote might do it. Then you can get back to the work at hand, knowing your audience is still with you.

I remember one speaker giving us a short break by saying, "I'm telling you the truth here. Sometimes the truth is painful. Like when a young mother showed me her new young baby—the most unattractive baby I had ever seen—and asked me if I thought it was cute. What could I say? The truth would hurt. So I said, 'He looks a lot like his father.'"

4. Humor can clarify obscure or complicated issues: Abraham Lincoln was a polished story-teller. It was a skill he honed as a lawyer travelling through the Eighth Judicial Circuit. He was probably the first President to use humor as a political and executive implement.

As he was campaigning for President his advisors sometimes implored him to use stories more. Anecdotes were effective, they argued, and could win him support and votes. Lincoln said, "I do not seek applause . . . nor to amuse the people. I want to convince them."

His anecdotes were not only convincing, but they also saved valuable time. He said, "I often avoid a long and useless discussion by others or a laborious explanation on my own part by a short story that illustrates my point of view."

Good humor has to be clear. It has to appeal to the listener and be understood. It must be easy to recognize and identify. The truth and reality of it have to be apparent. If not, the listener simply "doesn't get it."

That clarity, recognition, and understanding, though, work in reverse as well. Understanding the principles behind the joke can help a person understand your point of view.

I remember in the presidential debates of 1984, Mondale said to one of his adversaries, "Where's the beef?" That was a catch phrase from a popular TV commercial at the time. Mondale's quote got tremendous press and served him well. The people listening to the debate understood his point at once. He was saying, "You have all these policies, but there's no substance to any of them. Where's the beef?"

I remember a simple line that cut through a lot of technicalities, euphemisms, political diversions, and much else. It was during the Vietnam conflict. We had fighting men there, but they weren't supposed to be fighting men because it wasn't supposed to be a war.

The guys who were there were as uncomfortable as if it were a war. People were shooting at them, which reminded them of a war. To them, it looked like a duck, quacked like a duck, and waddled like a duck, but it was not allowed to be called a duck.

When Bob Hope came to entertain, he began his monologue by saying to the troops, "Hello, Advisors."

They were just two simple words, but the fellows in the audience knew what they said.

As executives, we often have to explain policies that are difficult to accept. It's not that the listeners can't understand, but the situation behind them may be too tangled to unravel. Especially in those cases, a wise selection of humor can illustrate the salient points.

I once listened to a manager give a pep talk to a group that had let down badly. Production had to improve or the entire line would be dropped and layoffs begun. The talk was factual, but also threatening. What had happened—and why—were beyond the scope of the lecture. But the manager made his bottom line point emphatically. He said, "I'm not saying all these things because your jobs are on the line. I'm saying them because mine is."

5. Humor helps your audience remember your points: No message is worth anything if the listeners leave it in the meeting room. Your audience has to take that message home with them, or at least, back to the office. Humor can help your listeners do that in two ways: First, it helps them remember what you said and, secondly, it helps them recall it when they need it.

Let me give you an example of what I mean. I had a friend once who was an incurable name dropper. Since we were all in show business, we would tell stories about stars we knew. My friend would always have a story about that same star after you told yours. It might not be a better story; it was just a story. It said, "I know that person, too."

When he was told that this habit was annoying, my friend accepted the criticism, but said, "I don't do it maliciously. It's just that I do know these people and your stories always remind me of another story." Then someone quoted Will Rogers's remark about a fellow he liked: "He's my favorite kind of musician. He knows how to play the ukulele, but he don't."

It made the point well, and it also served as a constant reminder. Each time my friend was prompted to tell a "topper" story, he remembered "not to play the ukulele."

Why is humor such a good reminder? Because good humor is fun, it stays with us. We always remember the good old days and forget the bad. Also, humor is graphic. A worthwhile story, joke, witticism, is not so much a collection of words as it is a picture in the mind of the listener.

That's why different people react to different jokes in different ways.

No two listeners paint the same mental image. Phyllis Diller's material has always been highly graphic. When she kids her husband's drinking, and she says, "Fang cut himself shaving this morning. He bled so badly his eyes cleared up," you can't help but form some sort of visual. You may see a man whose bloodshot eyes are gradually draining. You may laugh a bit louder if you picture the way you've looked on certain mornings. But you do form a picture, and pictures stay in our memory longer.

To illustrate this, here is a little experiment. I'll give you a list of ten 4-digit numbers. You can spend some time and try to memorize them, or you can estimate how long it would take you to remember them. Don't waste a lot of time on Part One of this experiment because it's Part Two that is enlightening.

Part One

Here are the numbers:

1. 3452
2. 7843
3. 9024
4. 7726
5. 8705
6. 2145
7. 3598
8. 4233
9. 4581
10. 3909

First, for Part One: if you did try to memorize those numbers, I'm sure it would take you some time, and you probably wouldn't remember them for too long. End of day, they'd be gone—certainly by tomorrow.

Part Two

For Part Two of this experiment, though, I'll give you another list of ten numbers, but I'll give you a graphic way of remembering them. I almost guarantee that you'll remember them easily. They'll remain with you all day, and probably tomorrow you'll be able to recall most of them, too.

Let's try it. Here are the numbers:

1. 1439
2. 1211
3. 4416
4. 5205
5. 1349
6. 2576
7. 6599
8. 5088
9. 5529
10. 2048

Before you start, I'd like you to memorize these visuals. They are picture words that rhyme with numbers, from one to ten. One is gun, two is shoe, three is tree, four is door, five is hive (a beehive), six is sticks, seven is heaven, eight is a gate, nine is a bottle of wine, ten is a hen. Memorizing those should take about half a minute.

Now, break down the four-digit numbers into combinations of two-digit numbers. For example, 1349 becomes 13-49 and so on. Then I'll give you pictures that suit the numbers. From that we'll paint a graphic picture that will remain in your head. The wilder and more bizarre the image is, the easier it will be to recall and the longer it will remain. Let's try it.

For number one, we picture a gun, but a unique gun—a blunderbuss. A person jumps out of a hiding place with the gun, but instead of threatening you, he forces you to take a vacation. The vacation signifies the number 14, for 14 days. So you picture yourself riding in a rickshaw around Hong Kong with Jack Benny. Why Jack Benny? Because he was always 39 years old. Hence, you get that image in your mind and you have the first number—1439.

Now (for two) we picture a large shoe, like the old lady who lived in a shoe. The door of the shoe opens and out rush the twelve disciples with numbers on their togas and helmets on their head. They're rushing out to play a football game. The significance? There are twelve disciples and eleven men on a football team. Hence, the second number is 1211.

Next is a tree (for three). Picture a pretty girl in an old-fashioned white dress swinging from a swing on the tree. However, she jumps up and starts firing western pistols. The guns are Colt-44's, and the girl is sweet sixteen. Therefore, the third image is 4416.

Four (door) is a pair of swinging doors to a western saloon. You walk through and start playing cards with a basketball team. The guys are so tall that you can hardly reach the card table. There are 52 cards in a deck and five men on a basketball team. Four equals 5205.

For five (hive), a black cat jumps out of a beehive and starts chasing some old westerners who are in the river panning for gold. It's a mad chase. The black cat is for the unlucky number 13, and the gold-panners are '49ers. Five equals 1349.

Next you picture a pile of twigs on a silver tray. The sticks represent six, and the silver tray is for 25, the silver anniversary. You hear faint music coming from the twigs. You move the twigs aside and see three tiny little men. They march around the tray. One plays the flute, another the drums, and the third proudly carries the American flag. They are the spirit of '76, representing the last two digits—76. Therefore six is 2576.

For seven you visualize the pearly gates of heaven. St. Peter has to open the gates quickly because an older gentleman with grey hair is coming through. He's being chased by an old-time train engine. The significance: The old man is 65, the traditional retirement age. The train is Engine 99. So, seven is 6599.

Eight is a beat-up old fence gate. You swing it open and discover a dazzling, gold piano. The gold represents 50, the golden anniversary. The piano means 88, the number of keys on the keyboard. Eight equals 5088.

Nine, you are drinking from a bottle of wine. You are sitting by the bottom of a roadway marker that reads 55. It's the speed warning by the side of the road. Along the roadway you see a bunch of down-and-out stockbrokers pushing apple carts. This represents the crash of '29. Therefore nine means 5529.

Finally, you see a very large hen (ten) walk into an open mine. In it a bunch of miners are playing pinochle. The miners represent the number 20, the last year you are a minor. Pinochle means 48 since there are only 48 cards in a pinochle deck. So ten is 2048.

I'm glad you persevered through this experiment with me. Test yourself, though. Ask yourself what the sixth number is. Do you remember what you visualized when you thought of a gate for eight?

You should be able to recall most of these four-digit numbers with little or no study—nothing beyond the brief reading of the paragraphs contained in the text. Notice what has happened. With crazy, zany, yet graphic word pictures I tricked you into a commendable feat of memorization. I got you to commit to memory 40 digits in sequence—something that you probably wouldn't do otherwise.

You can do the same for your listeners with graphic, funny, *memorable* illustrations. You can dupe them into remembering what they don't particularly want to remember—but you want them to. That's the power that a judicious use of humor can give a speaker.

This is, of course, a gimmick, but a serious one. Most memory systems are based on graphic visualization. Picturing images does enhance the memory.

Humor not only gives you a graphic image to help your memory, but it also gives you another idea to relate to. That aids recall also. For example, let me ask you if you know the square root of three. Do you remember the birth year of George Washington? I know both. I've remembered them since my sophomore year in high school. I couldn't forget them even if I wanted to. Why? Because some astute teacher once told me that Washington was born in the square root of three. That one remark enabled me to remember that Washington's birth year is 1732 and the square root of three is 1.732. What's even more remarkable is that I didn't know either one before he said that.

Can you name all five Great Lakes? I would always forget at least one until an instructor told our class that if we owned two homes we would remember them. That was a hint she dropped; we had to do the detective work on our own. Then one of us hit on the solution and probably none of us has forgotten it since. "Homes" is an acronym for the five lakes—Huron, Ontario, Michigan, Erie, and Superior.

If you want people to remember what you say, give them graphic stories to illustrate your main points. They'll stay locked in the mind longer. In fact, they're difficult to forget, just as you probably can't forget that a black cat jumped out of a beehive and chased some guys panning for gold. And the fifth number was 1349.

6. Humor can relax tension: A toy existed when I was a kid called the "Chinese Finger Torture," or something exotic like that. It was simply a cylinder woven from some fibrous material. You'd insert both forefingers into it and then discover that the harder you tried to pull them out, the tighter the fiber would bind together, locking your fingers in.

None of us, of course, stayed trapped forever (well, maybe one or two kids from the neighborhood, I don't know), but the principle is interesting. The more you resisted, the tighter it became. Tension in an auditorium is like that.

It's like when you make a social faux pas—say something you shouldn't say, for example—the more you try to cover, the more embarrassing it becomes.

Tension is a part of public speaking. It's especially prevalent in business meetings because existing tension is often involved in the reason for getting together in the first place. There are meetings to boost lagging production, meetings to lift failing sales figures, meetings to decide whether to go with product A or product B, meetings to decide whether Sales or Marketing was at fault in the recent fiasco, and so on.

Tension, if allowed to continue, can create a distraction for both the speaker and the listeners. The speaker can certainly be aware of it, intimidated by it, and affected by it. The listeners are thinking about the unresolved issue instead of listening to the message. So, it's best to confront it, face it head-on, and dismiss it. Humor is a very effective way of doing that.

I remember one of my first confrontations at work involved a new drafting technique that I introduced. The manufacturing representative resisted it—hard. He and I got to butting heads so furiously that our manager had to step in to resolve the issue. When he called us into his office, I was eager to prove that I wasn't at fault and the marketing rep was just as prepared to show that it wasn't his fault, either. Our manager stopped us cold.

"I want all of us to relax and work together on this problem," he said. "I'm the one who's at fault here. I hired both of you."

7. Humor can defuse an adversary's attack: I was playing a singles tennis match with a good friend one day when his wife and her girlfriend approached the court. His wife shouted, "Would you like to play mixed doubles?" My heart sank. It wasn't a sexist reaction, believe me. I enjoy good mixed doubles play, but these ladies weren't at our level of tennis. I was looking forward to a good, competitive singles contest.

While I mentally struggled to find an excuse that would be believable and inoffensive—but effective—my friend simply shouted back, "Life is too short."

The women laughed and went to the next court for some singles of their own.

My heart had skipped a beat. The "fight or run" adrenaline had kicked into my system; my mind went blank; my tongue swelled up. I became a helpless, slithering wimp. Yet he used just a dash of wit, and the problem was deflected.

Humor can have a paralyzing effect on an opponent, or perhaps it would be more accurate to say that it can allow an opponent to have a paralyzing effect on himself. It's a passive form of combat, so to speak.

Some forms of martial arts use that strategy. They allow an adversary's weight, force, strength, and momentum to be used against him. Rather than oppose the attack, you flow with it. That's the secret of humor as a defense mechanism.

A good example is Ronald Reagan during the 1984 Presidential campaigns. As we mentioned before, age was a major issue. It wouldn't go away because his opponents wouldn't let it go away.

The Reagan camp could have countered with fact-filled rebuttals, because many studies indicate that age doesn't affect mental capacity. However, these arguments would only have invited counter-argument and the troublesome issue would have remained center stage.

Reagan's response was to de-activate the issue with humor. He did age jokes on himself as often as he could. When his opponents tried to bring up the issue, it was dead—deflated. Reagan had done it—himself. He effectively joked the annoying argument out of existence.

Here are a few of the gags he did on himself:

Some people reminded Reagan that if he were reelected, he would be 76 years old when he left office. Reagan replied,

"Well, Andrew Jackson left the White House at the age of seventy-five and he was still quite vigorous. I know because he told me."

Speaking to the Gridiron Club, Reagan noted that the organization had been founded in 1885. "How disappointed I was," he said, "when you didn't invite me the first time."

Reagan once told a group of doctors, "We've made so many advances in my lifetime. For example, I have lived ten years longer than my life expectancy when I was born—a source of annoyance to a great many people."

8. Humor can get results: Some arguments can go on forever. As kids in Philadelphia, my buddies and I used to debate endlessly which was the better team—the Athletics or the Phillies. Was Robin Roberts a better pitcher than Bobby Shantz? Some 35 years later, we can still get hot under the collar during these discussions.

Business disagreements can last almost as long. The basic questions can get fogged in by egos, personality clashes, departmental restrictions, and who-knows-what-all. Competent business logic surrenders to pettiness and nothing gets resolved.

Humor can help clarify these situations. The brightness and innate logic of humor can often bring a muddled situation into distinct focus.

We once had a small, but lingering strike where I worked. Most of the issues had been reasonably resolved, but the union and management negotiators now were waging a power struggle. Neither one would compromise, so the company and the workers suffered because of their stubbornness.

Each day the union issued a bulletin "explaining the facts." It didn't explain any facts at all. It just slung mud at the company negotiators. It was so obviously sarcastic and slanted that even the union members were embarrassed by it.

Then the company team would issue a rebuttal bulletin. It would out-sarcastic the union sheet. Now the union members would rally behind their besieged officials.

The union would then publish another page or two and the problem would continue see-sawing.

I was the supervisor of the striking workers, so the union team invited me to the strategy sessions. They asked my advice. I told them a story about a talk I had heard a college football player give. He was a very mediocre offensive lineman, but he had played a great game against a consensus All-American that weekend. He told us about it:

"If I tried to block this guy out of the play, he would just toss me aside and rush into the play. I wasn't good enough to control him. So, I started blocking him *into* the play. Then he'd toss me aside and run away from the play and leave a big hole for our runners to go through.

"He was too smart to put up with that for very long. When he caught on, I would sometimes block him into the play and other times I would block him out of the play.

"It got to where he would just guess, and half the time he guessed wrong. When he guessed wrong and ran away from the play, I'd just let him run."

That's how the kid had an outstanding day of football against a far superior ball-player.

I told our company negotiating team that the union, with their ill-conceived personal attacks, were running the wrong way. When they did, we should just let them run. Replying in kind was uniting the union members against us.

When our General Manager convinced the negotiating team that they should swallow their pride and not respond to each attack, the union membership forced their negotiators to accept what was actually a reasonable settlement in the first place.

9. Humor can motivate and inspire: Wit has such a well-defined logic, making its points forcefully and clearly, that many excellent speakers also use it to motivate.

John Heisman, the Georgia Tech football coach after whom the Heisman trophy is named, would make his point very demonstrably at the beginning of each football practice season. He'd hold up a ball and announce, "This is a football. It's an elongated spheroid, inflated with air and covered with an outer layer of coarsely grained leather. Heaven help the first man who fumbles it."

Knute Rockne, the famed Notre Dame football coach, was reportedly a bombastic halftime orator. His locker room pep talks were classics of motivational fire and brimstone.

At one game in which Notre Dame was being decidedly outplayed, the team trudged into the locker room at half-time and waited. They knew their coach was going to lean into them heavily, and they were prepared for a loud harangue. But Rockne never showed up. They waited and wondered, but still no coach. Finally, just before they were called back out to the stadium, the coach opened the door and said, "Oh, excuse me. I was looking for the Notre Dame football team."

Notre Dame won the game.

Finally, here's a little story that doesn't fall into any of the other categories. It was humor that certainly came too late to motivate or inspire. However, I enjoyed it so much that I think it's worth ending the chapter with.

John McKay coached the University of Southern California one day in a losing cause. He must have felt his players let him down, because after the game he went to the locker room and said, "The team bus leaves in half an hour. Those who need showers, take 'em."

CHAPTER THREE

The Dignity of Humor

Let's flashback to our entertaining flight attendant from Chapter One. You remember, the young lady who used a few jokes to get us all to listen to her safety instructions. Let's get annoyed at her.

After all, this is a message that is mandated by the FAA. It's not to be treated lightly. It's not to be ridiculed, played with, or made sport of.

There are many people who could be incensed at this employee's actions. She defiled the sanctity of a serious message. She did a disservice to the passengers who have a right to a message free of capricious editorializing. She diminished the dignity of all flight attendants, most of whom are serious, hard-working employees, dedicated to the comfort and safety of their customers.

Boy, are we pissed off.

Suppose, though, there had been an emergency. Would you have preferred to have had a dignified, august lecture on safety, or one that every passenger heard and absorbed?

Let's look at some of the possible complaints against this humorous approach and respond to them.

"It makes light of the instructions." Well, it didn't make light of them. This young lady kidded the passengers. We all enjoyed it when she said we were a handsome crowd, and we got a kick out of turning around so the folks in the back could see us. We thought it was funny when she kidded our travelling companions by saying, "If you're travelling with children or people acting like children." She teased her own airline, or more accurately all airlines: seatbacks *are*

uncomfortable when they're in their full, upright, and locked position. She poked fun at her own colleagues by pointing out that when they put on an oxygen mask, they didn't get one strand of hair out of place.

She kidded many things, but not the instructions. They were important to her. They were the reason she was forcing us to listen.

"She was being disrespectful." To whom? To what? The passengers enjoyed it—the overwhelming majority of them. We enjoyed it so much, that the good feeling continued throughout the entire flight.

Her airline must have approved of it. I've heard other flight attendants give similar safety lectures since then, so I'm positive the authorities have given their blessing.

The FAA couldn't object. They want this lecture heard, and it was heard.

"I don't have much confidence in a person who would stoop to such shenanigans when she should be taking her job more seriously." Quite the opposite: This young lady took her job seriously enough to force a group of reluctant listeners to pay attention to her. She knew we had never listened before, but we listened today. She captured us.

She knew enough about the situation, her job, and us, to get done what had to be done. I felt quite secure travelling with her. If a serious problem did arise, I believe she would have handled it with the same confidence and sense of humor. Isn't that the kind of image we're all looking for?

There are those who criticize all humor. Laughter and fun belong at parties and in nightclubs, they say. Others feel that any comedy, except on the professional stage, is undignified.

Certainly, I don't mean to give carte blanche to all forms of humor. I'm not suggesting that anything that gets a laugh is appropriate in your office or in your business speaking. Certain forms of comedy are annoying anywhere and some are unsuitable for executives. We'll discuss them later in the chapter. It's the resistance to levity of any kind in the business world that is worth analyzing here.

Many people have that prejudice. Laughter in the office is wrong, they feel. "We are there to work, and work should not be fun."

Recent studies are showing that managers have begun to appreciate the productive qualities of humor in the office. With a sense of humor, workers get along better, promote morale within the office, can accept managerial direction better. A sense of humor is high on their priorities in searching for managerial talent, too.

Why should humor be suspect in the office? Well, humor is generally honest. And sometimes that is hard to take.

There's a story about a woman on a train with her infant. A passenger looks at it and says, "That's the ugliest baby I've ever seen in my life." The mother is infuriated. She physically attacks the transgressor. Finally the conductor breaks up the fracas and tries to calm everyone down. He says, "Sit down, lady. Relax and take it easy. I'll get a banana for your monkey, and everything'll be all right."

Because humor is so incisive and so relentlessly rational, many people don't want to permit it to affect their thinking. "I've made up my mind," they insist. "Don't confuse me with facts." A manager who is convinced that his image is proper, but his competence is suspect may insist on perfect decorum in his office. "Let's stick with style because exposing substance could get me canned."

Those who are not afraid of the truth are not afraid of humor.

Someone once told me that "the truth will never hurt you." I don't buy that. Anyone who has ever seen my tennis game knows that telling the truth about it can seriously hurt my ego.

How about someone who wants to be a great football player, but just doesn't have the skills? Doesn't it hurt to inform him?

A young lady may want to be a famous fashion model. She simply doesn't have the bone structure. Isn't it painful for her to discover this?

You want to be the CEO of your firm. Isn't it distressing to discover that you probably never will be?

Sure, all of these things hurt. Assuming, though, that they're all true, isn't it better to find them out and redirect your ambitions rather than lead a fruitless life? It's not the truth that goes on hurting; it's the resistance to the truth.

Sure, my tennis game is lousy, but I continue to have fun. I just play lousier players who haven't yet realized how terrible they are.

Once I accept the reality of my tennis game, I can have fun with it. My friends can kid me. I enjoy that. I once was playing net in a doubles match and my opponent hit a shot right past me, down the alley. It was a clear winner. I pointed my finger at him in mock retaliation. "I hold a grudge for a long time," I said. He answered, "The way you play tennis, I imagine you'd have to."

The first requirement for a solid, dependable, there-when-you-need-it sense of humor is a confident self-image. If you can look at yourself honestly and like what you see, you can allow others to look at you critically. You can have a sense of humor about what you see and what they see.

I was going to give a talk about this once and I prepared a statement like this: "As I look around this room, I know that I'm better than half the people in this room, and not as good as the other half." At first I thought it was a pertinent, meaningful line; then on reflection I realized it was dumb.

There is no measure of who is better than whom. Is John McEnroe better than me because he hits the tennis ball harder, or am I better than him because I can write more funny lines faster? Is the big guy in the third row of my audience better than me because he's built better, or is the guy in the 15th row better than both of us because he's got a higher IQ? What basis do you use to evaluate the worth of individuals?

I'm not better than any of the people in my audience nor any worse. We're all just different. We all have pluses and minuses that total up to an individual. When you're happy with that individual, you can be justly proud of the pluses, and have a sense of humor about the minuses.

Let's quickly see how a solid self-image helps your sense of humor and helps you in the long run. You're at a party or in a club and some stranger calls you "Hook-nose." Now this angers you. It angers you mostly because he's right.

So, what do you do? You challenge him. Why? Because that's another one of those misconceptions that we've come to accept. A macho man doesn't allow himself to be belittled. He fights for his dignity.

Suppose, though, you have a powerful, yet honest, self-image. Sure, you have a hook-nose. So did George Washington. In fact, they put his on the one-dollar bill. They carved it into Mt. Rushmore, right near Abraham Lincoln who had a pretty big schnozzola himself.

Yeah, you've got a hook-nose. It's the same one your wife fell in love with. Your kids aren't going to throw you out of the house because of it. That beak of yours may just add the right touch of character to your features.

Even if you consider it a liability, it's still only a part of the picture. You've presumably got so much else going for you that it overshadows this drawback. People like comedian David Brenner even kid themselves about things like that. Brenner says, "When I was a kid, my nose was so big I thought it was a third arm."

You can take the hook-nose and assign it either a plus or a minus value. That's up to you. It's not up to some stranger. Therefore, what that person says should have no effect on your personal evaluation. If you have a strong enough self image, it won't.

Some of our greatest leaders show us how to have a sense of humor about ourselves. Lincoln used to tell a story about meeting two elderly ladies while he was out riding one day. He frightened them a bit. The one woman said angrily, "Sir, you are the ugliest man alive." Lincoln said, "I can't help that, M'am." She said, "You could at least stay home."

There's also the story about the time Churchill reportedly had too much to drink. A woman at the party chided him, saying, "Mr. Churchill, you're drunk." He replied, "And you, Madam, are ugly. But tomorrow morning I'll be sober."

Some feel that levity, if not the arch-enemy of dignity, is at least a threat to it.

Well, they took Abraham Lincoln seriously. They took Will Rogers seriously enough to ask him to run for President. He refused. He was a comedian; not a politician. I think he enjoyed more getting his laughs on purpose.

They take Bob Hope seriously, too. He has dined with kings, queens, presidents, prime ministers, heads of state. He is sophisticated, urbane, dignified—and funny.

Again, the conflict between humor and dignity arises when we try to present a false veneer as genuine.

I used to play golf on the public links in Philadelphia many years ago (my golf was worse than my tennis). Several of us were on the starting tee bright and early one Saturday morning. It was so early, in fact, that the first hole was shrouded with morning mist. You could only see about the length of a mediocre tee shot.

As we crowded around, waiting for our startup time to be called, a foursome approached the first tee. They were gorgeous. They had all the proper equipment and their golf clothes were expensive and matching. They were too splendid for our lowly public course.

Then they teed off. The first shot went about 70 yards. The next went about 30 to the right. They just kept walking along the fairway swinging at the ball. We all watched stunned as they each took about 4 slices at the golf ball before mercifully disappearing into the mist.

When they were out of sight, we laughed uncontrollably. They were dressed for golf, but they weren't prepared for golf. You see, the costume is not the ability. Dressing like Jack Nicklaus doesn't improve your backswing. Looking like the Masters Champion doesn't get you from tee to green in regulation. In fact, it can make you look even more absurd.

The accoutrements of dignity are not dignity. There are those who would look dignified, and there are those who have dignity. They're not always the same.

Mortimer Levitt, founder of the Custom Shops and a very wealthy man, said of class, "Arriving in a Rolls Royce is not class. That's the accoutrements of class. Real class is how you treat your chauffeur."

Let's take a look at the forms of humor that might be harmful to a business speaker.

1. Slapstick or physical humor: This generally doesn't belong in the business speaker's repertoire. Milton Berle used to get a lot of laughs and big money dressing up in women's clothes and walking on his ankles. I don't think the manager of sales should open an employee meeting with this shtick.

2. Gratuitous insults: Many professional comics rely on the insult joke. Don Rickles is probably the outstanding example. His insults are obvious. There are others who do more insidious insulting and for no good reason. We writers call this gratuitous. There is a joke in an insult, therefore you do the insult to get the joke. It's not prompted or motivated by any logic.

Business leaders should avoid this type of humor at all costs, because it shows a lack of sensitivity. One manager I worked with years ago used these types of jokes constantly. He'd insult other managers and other departments. We'd all wince when we heard him. It wasn't that we disagreed with his conclusions; we just hated his presentation. It was cruel, vicious, and unfair. It showed us that he didn't think things through before speaking.

3. Put-down humor: This dangerous form of wit says to an audience, "I'm better than you, and don't you forget it." It boasts of being superior—whatever that is—richer, more sophisticated, at a higher management level, whatever. It inflates your own standing and deflates your audience. It may get laughs, but it won't win anyone over. It antagonizes people.

4. Sarcasm: This is another dangerous, insidious form of humor. It pretends to be wit, but it's really viciousness in disguise. An audience can feel the difference.

Will Rogers said it best: "If there's no malice in your heart, there can't be none in your humor."

The acid test here is what you intend to accomplish with your wit. If you're trying to make a point, you can be caustic. If you're trying to wound, don't.

Note: None of the above rules out insult humor. When this is used well, and wisely, it can be a powerful tool. There are ways to insure that your insults are harmless—more fun than fang. We'll talk about those in a later chapter. For now, though, realize that humor is a powerful tool. It shouldn't be used to hurt.

---

5. Questionable taste: This covers material that might be considered dirty, ethnic, or sarcastic, as well as hurtful insult humor. Remember that the humor you use reflects on you, just as the clothes you wear do. It's never worth offending anyone with your wit. The best rule of thumb is: if you're in doubt, don't.

6. Humor that contradicts your personality: If your humor really is a reflection of you, everything you say, even in fun, should be consistent. Why? Because you're using humor as a business tool. It serves no purpose to confuse your listeners. They would wonder which is the real you—the serious one or the witty one. There's no confusion if you're consistent.

7. Humor that contradicts your philosophy: As an executive, as a business leader, you have a philosophy. You have a set of ethics that you adhere to. Any humor you use should be consistent with that. Humor used judiciously can gain respect for any speaker. But humor that contradicts your thinking can wreck people's respect for you. Be sure that what you say in jest is what you would say seriously. People are going to hear *everything* you say. What you say with humor may be heard even more clearly than the rest. Be sure it's what you want to say.

In working for Bob Hope and other comics, it's amazing how much funny material they just won't do. They won't permit themselves to. Even for professional funny people, image is important.

As a youngster I used to listen to a radio personality. He had a kiddie show and I was among his biggest fans. One night, he mentioned my name and told me to look under the sofa for a birthday gift. I did, and sure enough there was a watch there. I was thrilled and mystified. I had no idea that my parents had called in and told him what to say.

One night I listened to him as he said a sincere good-bye to all of us youngsters; then he said something else. He didn't know the mike was still live. He said, "Well, that should take care of the little bastards for another day."

That was the last time I ever heard him on radio.

CHAPTER FOUR

Overcoming the Fear of Humor

When I was a writer on *The Carol Burnett Show*, we had a guest star who wasn't too pleased with the sketch that we had written for him. He was a respected, talented dramatic actor who had a hit detective series on the air. He was also a fine gentleman—very professional, and a delight to work with. He just didn't care for this particular sketch.

He respectfully requested that we replace the sketch, or at least, replace him in it. But Carol, the staff, and the rest of us thought it was hilarious and persuaded him to stick with it a little longer. He did, but his heart wasn't in it.

He rehearsed with little gusto, simply reading the lines—no enthusiasm, no flair, no emotion. Rehearsals went poorly.

On tape night, this gentleman was depressed. He didn't want to go out there and do this sketch, but by now it was too late to avoid it. When he got his music cue, he walked onto the set, still reluctant. He was determined to do this piece of material bravely before a live audience, endure their indifference, and then walk around backstage with an unspoken "I told you so" written across his features.

He delivered his first line and it got giant laughs from the audience. The crowd bought the concept, thought it was funny, and roared.

This gentleman's eyes were a sub-plot in themselves. At first they were diverted in shame from the audience. At the sound of the laughter, they lifted up in disbelief. He looked at the audience openly, as if to reassure himself that they weren't laughing at someone running naked up and down the aisles. When he saw that he was a comedy hit, his eyes lit up. They sparkled. He was rejuvenated with new energy, and he performed the rest of the sketch like a marvelously broad burlesque ham. He was magnificent, and he had the greatest time of his performing life. He had discovered comedy.

Many people fear humor. And with good reason, too. In 1833, British actor Edmund Kean was near death. A friend at his bedside whispered comfortingly, "How are you doing?" Kean's famous answer was: "Dying is easy; comedy is difficult."

When I give seminars to speakers and comedy writers, I hear this echoed constantly, though less dramatically.

"I can't do comedy."

"I just can't tell a joke."

"I can never remember jokes."

"Every time I try to be funny, I fail."

I sympathize with these complaints, but I don't believe any of them. Oh, I believe that the people are sincere. I believe that they've tried humor and failed. But who hasn't?

In any humor seminar I give, people ask, "What are some of the common mistakes people make in using humor?" My first reply is, "They quit too soon." Beginning writers abandon the joke line too quickly. They stop writing the routine before they've exhausted the possibilities. Speakers jump ship after the first abortive attempt.

None of them are giving humor—a difficult art form—a fair chance.

Golf is not easy, either. Yet, people don't take a few swings and say, "I can't play this game,"—"I can't master the swing,"—"I've tried to break 90, but just can't do it." Not at all. They take their lessons, get their weekend starting times, and continue to play. And they get better.

They could make the same strides with humor if they would give it a fair chance.

Let's analyze a few of those objections.

You can't do comedy? Of course you can. Everybody can. You can't do it the first time out, maybe, but neither could you hit a golf ball correctly on the first swing. You couldn't drive the first time you sat behind the wheel, either. Hell, you had trouble walking when you first started, too.

You can't tell a joke? Don't be so critical of yourself. If you can make a point with logic, if you can "sell" your point of view to clients or fellow workers, if you can inspire and motivate people with your lectures, you can tell a joke.

Our guest star on the *Burnett Show* could work the emotions of an audience with his dramatic training. Those same skills worked when he tried comedy. It surprised him, but it didn't surprise us. We knew from dealing with comedy week after week, that more people can handle it than realize they can handle it.

Remember, though, that this man destroyed several rehearsals with his negative approach. You, too, can influence the results with your attitude. Delivering humor with "I just can't tell a joke" in the back of your mind, hurts. Try to go into each effort "full out." Hold nothing back and you may discover with delight, as our reluctant comedy guest star did, that the audience won't hold back either.

You can never remember jokes? So what? Who says you have to? When you deliver a speech, you generally have time to prepare it, don't you? Well, that should give you ample time to research a dash of humor, too.

You're not being challenged to a duel of wits with Milton Berle. You don't have to toss out rapid fire insults like Don Rickles. You needn't ad-lib in a constant, funny stream-of-consciousness like Robin Williams or Jonathan Winters. You simply need a clever quote, a cute aside, or an amusing anecdote to illustrate your main points.

Also, you are permitted to use notes. So why worry about remembering jokes?

Every time you try to be funny, you fail? This reminds me of the reply Victor Borge gave when an interviewer asked if he had played piano all his life. Borge said, "Certainly not. I'm not dead yet." Maybe every time you tried to be funny, you failed—until now. Now is when you're going to start trying it, get better each time, and eventually learn how to use humor effectively.

If you're really honest with yourself, you have to admit that you can be entertaining. That's as important as anything else you'll learn in the following pages.

One final encouragement, though, before we move on. Any fear of humor you have must be tempered with the reality of what you're trying to do. Edmund Kean was right; comedy is difficult. But you who are reading this book are not trying to become comedians. You're not stepping to the podium to do a 90-minute nightclub act like Bill Cosby. You don't have to do a solid hour of one-liners like Bob Hope. You are simply trying to augment the power of your message with humor. There's a tremendous difference.

Why are people afraid of humor?

Humor is powerful: Like electricity, fire, or any source of power, humor can do harm. I've been hurt by it a few times. In one company I worked in a department that was a bit off the wall. We were known as the "zanies" of the plant, and I don't say that with pride. In one of my monologues I did a little routine about it. Jokes like, "Our supervisor left the office for a while the other day. By the time he got back, we had let all the sand out of the sandbox."

I delivered this routine in front of fellow workers and representatives of management. Afterwards, my supervisor came to me and said, "You've just killed my career at this plant."

I'm not sure I destroyed his career, but I did hurt him with that routine. It was ill-advised, not thought out, and it did harm. It offended him, first of all, and it probably did reflect on his record.

Yes, humor can hurt. However, that needn't produce fear; it should generate respect. There's a difference. Normal people don't fear electricity; we respect it. We don't stick knives into toasters, we don't repair lights or outlets without first switching off the power, we don't replace burned out fuses with a penny. But we're not terrified of turning on the light switch, and we don't cringe each time we change channels on the TV.

As with any potentially harmful force, we need to learn what can cause the damage and then deal with it. The hurt from humor can stem from either of two sources: malice or ignorance.

Humor can be used maliciously. That's what children do when they taunt others. That's what we can do when we use comedy or sarcasm to antagonize others. That's what union and management were doing in those strike flyers I mentioned earlier.

The remedy is simply to vow not to use humor as a weapon.

Ignorance is a little more precarious. We generally know when we're being malicious; we don't know when we're ignorant.

There is some ignorance that we'll never be able to do anything about. Knowledge simply isn't available to us. For instance, I visited a factory and did a humorous routine about the age of the building. It was quite old; everyone knew it was ancient; and they had kidded themselves about it often. But the gags didn't play. Why? Because the employees had just gotten word—and it wasn't yet available for public knowledge—that the factory would be shut down because it was effectively obsolete.

The "harmless" one-liners now had a painful barb to them, but I had no way of knowing what had happened.

Generally, though, our ignorance is remediable. When I kidded my supervisor, I should have realized that it would paint him as incompetent. I didn't. That was my fault.

The solution is to think through any humor you use. Learn to hear it through the mind of your listeners. If this humor you're using were said about you, or your work, or your associates, would you be offended by it? If you would, don't say it.

Humor is not easy: My manager always reminded me that "simplicity is the product of thought." Good, effortless, natural flowing humor is the end result of lots of hard work.

I have worked with many of the top names in professional comedy and I can guarantee that effort goes into their humor. I have worked on staff for a performer who might deliver 20 comedy lines on camera. We wrote over 3000 to get those 20. I've been at meetings where one line needed replacing before a sketch could be taped. The writing staff might stay at the typewriter until 2 o'clock in the morning in order to have the line ready for the next day's taping. I've written ad-libs for comedians where we had to write a different line for all possible contingencies. Would the guest star say this? We'd answer with that. Would the guest star not say this? We'd reply with a different line. Would the guest star not show up? We'd have a line for that, too.

Humor requires homework and effort. We have to research, write, and rehearse our delivery. People like Robin Williams and Jonathan Winters seem to be able to do it spontaneously; the rest of us, even the top professionals, have to work at it. To try to do it without that effort, dooms our comedy to failure.

But wait a minute! If it's that difficult and requires so much effort, why should we even attempt it? Especially since we're not pros.

First of all, because it is a powerful tool. We've already discussed the merits of humor in business communication. A good executive is not going to reject such enormous benefit simply because it requires some work.

Second, the response to humor is immediate and honest. You've probably been in clubs where a singer performed badly. Still, at the end of the number, the audience politely applauded. They can't be that gracious with bad comics. They can't force laughter.

The flip side of that, though, is the benefit for the speaker. When humor works—when it hits an audience—the listeners can't disguise that either.

Many professional business speakers insist on evaluation cards. They want to know exactly how the audience rated their performance. Professional humorists don't care about evaluation cards. Anybody who is doing humor knows exactly how the audience rates that performance. The reaction can't be hidden and it can't be faked.

So when using humor well and wisely, you control the audience instead of vice-versa. That's a powerful implement to have with you at the podium.

Third, and we've touched on this already, you don't have to get big, sustained laughs. You're not trying for a career on the comedy stage. You're only looking for a touch of wit to strengthen your speaking. So, do expect to work at your humor, but that work should be proportionate to the amount of humor you'll be using.

For those of you who do have a genuine fear of humor, here's a step-by-step remedy:

1. Go gradually: Try to conquer your fear in small doses. Don't load your next speech with stories, one-liners, anecdotes, and quotes. Be satisfied with one amusing moment. Aim for just that. When you're satisfied that you can get that chuckle when and where you want it, then you can go for two, three, and eventually as many as you like.

2. Research one good piece of material: Make a concerted effort to find just one good laugh-getter. It can be a quote, a one-liner, or a good story. But read, research, ask other speakers what they've had luck with, and get one piece of material that *you* are convinced will work.

3. Rework the material to your satisfaction: Rarely will you find a piece of humorous material that you can do "as is." In other words, if you find an anecdote in *Reader's Digest*, it won't be in your words. It will be in *Reader's Digest* words. You now have to work with it until it sounds comfortable coming from your lips. Change the speech patterns. Change the "he says-she says." Make it sound like you.

Usually, it's just a matter of changing something from a literary form to a more conversational style. But it should be *your* conversational style.

4. Rehearse your delivery: Now that you've rewritten your story so that it indeed sounds like *your story*, you have to learn to say it like it's your story. That takes rehearsal time. Say it aloud. Hear how it sounds coming from you. Repeat it so often that when you begin to tell the story, the rest of it falls off your lips.

I once worked with a major motion picture star. For a while he was the biggest box office draw in the world. When he came to our first script reading, I was stunned to find that he was almost illiterate. He couldn't read the script as quickly as the rest of the cast. It was painful to sit through rehearsal. Yet, when the cameras were turned on, this gentleman recited each line flawlessly. Because he had so much trouble reading, he rehearsed with added diligence. That's why he performed so well.

So, whether you fear humor or not, it won't hurt to practice it to perfection.

5. Tell your story often: Now try your story with an audience. Tell it to friends. Tell it to anyone who will listen. You'll get the honest feedback that you need.

Each time you tell it you may learn a little more about the telling of it. You may change the way you tell it. In any case, you'll get better and better as you get more and more confident in the telling.

If you follow these steps with just one piece of material (no matter how tiny—it may just be a quotation from some famous person), you'll learn the process. It will become easier when you repeat it with another piece of humor and another. Gradually, you'll build up a repertoire and overcome that unnecessary fear.

CHAPTER FIVE

Humor and the Business Executive

I especially need a sense of humor because there are times in my life when I do dumb things. To paraphrase some anonymous humorist, "I'm quick to laugh at myself, if only to beat somebody else to the punch."

A medical group hired me as a luncheon speaker for their convention in Tahoe. They arranged my flight into Reno where they had me picked up by limousine for the hour ride to the convention hotel. However, right before my luncheon speech, they asked if they could make alternate arrangements to get me to the airport for my return flight. The limo, they said, was too expensive.

I didn't mind losing the limousine, but I did have a tight connection at the airport because of another speaking engagement. They said they had arranged for a shuttle to the airport.

Now I was concerned. I had used the shuttle once before in Tahoe and it stopped anywhere and everywhere. One time I remember we stopped at a supermarket to pick up a young lady who had just finished her weekly shopping. She had two children and several bags of groceries with her. When we reached her house, the rest of us on the shuttle helped her unload both kids and groceries. Because of my tight schedule, I thought the shuttle was out of the question.

My hosts had no alternate plans, and I lost my temper. "Forget about making any plans for me," I said. "I'll get to the airport myself. This is too important to me, and you folks don't seem to be concerned about details. I'll get to the airport myself, thank you."

Despite my irritation, the luncheon talk went well. At the end of it,

I asked if there was anyone going to the Reno airport immediately after lunch. A doctor volunteered to drive me there, and we had a pleasant ride.

I arrived with very little time to spare, thanked the doctor, and rushed to the check-in desk. "Am I on time to make this flight?" I asked. The girl behind the counter smiled and said, "You'd be in plenty of time except for one thing." "Except for what?" I barked. "Except you're at the wrong airport."

I was at the Reno airport; my return flight was scheduled to leave from the Tahoe airport, which was only a ten-minute drive from the hotel. I could have comfortably made it on the shuttle even if we did have to help a few people with their shopping bags.

In Tahoe I only made a fool of myself before strangers. The rest of the time I act dumb with my family. That's much worse; you have to see them every day.

The trumpet fiasco started when one of my children began to tire of music lessons. Like a good parent, I insisted on a practice session. Reluctantly, my offspring obeyed and we listened to scales being played badly on the trumpet. Each note had a ring of resentment to it.

When the practice time mercifully ended, my youngster asked me for help getting the trumpet back in the case. The mouthpiece was jammed onto the instrument.

I tried to pull the thing off but couldn't. We both tried to pull, one holding the horn, the other tugging on the mouthpiece. It wouldn't budge. The more I struggled with it, the angrier I became. I figured in a display of spiteful revenge, the ten-year old had purposely jammed this thing into the trumpet.

I got out my tool box. I put a thin piece of metal into the trumpet from the bell and tried to bang the mouthpiece out from the inside. I tapped it with a hammer, but still couldn't loosen that damned mouthpiece.

I banged a little harder. When I looked to see if I was loosening the part that was wedged in, I saw that the piece of metal was tearing through the side of the instrument. Now I couldn't get the piece of metal out.

So I inserted another piece of metal, a long file, to unwedge the first piece of metal. I lost that into the trumpet and couldn't get it out.

Now I was not only mad at my youngster, but at my own stupidity, and at whoever designed trumpets in the first place.

I became irrational, frightened my child, and did a lot of damage to an innocent horn.

When my temper quieted down, I realized that I now had to go to a music store and act nonchalant while asking a man to repair a trumpet with a sizable gash in its side and 4 or 5 pieces of metal and tubing wedged inside it. I hoped he wouldn't ask.

He didn't. He just stared at me in wonder. Then he explained what he would have to do. He'd have to weld a new part onto the trumpet to replace the torn metal. The instrument would be usable, but not equal in quality to the original. He'd also have to disassemble the horn to see if the offending metal had done any internal damage. The whole repair job would cost about $150. I said that would be all right.

I wasn't happy with my embarrassment, nor with the expense. The worst was yet to come, though. The repairman then said, "First of all, I'll have to get a mouthpiece pull to get this thing off." With a simple little device and perhaps 20 seconds of effort, he pulled that mouthpiece off just like taking a stick of gum out of the wrapper.

With just a touch of common sense and a phone call to a music shop, I could have saved myself $150 and some respect.

I might get a little more sympathy in this last anecdote of the trilogy, but not much. After a supposedly routine medical exam, I found that I had a problem that required heart surgery. As a precaution until the surgery, I had to wear a patch on my body with medication on it that was absorbed topically, through the skin.

I wasn't much fun to be around during that time. First of all, I was angered that I had a problem; I was comparatively young, ate well, kept myself in good shape with a reasonable amount of exercise and just couldn't understand why I needed repair work. In other words, "Why me?" Second, I hated this medicine. It had annoying side effects, and it was awkward. No matter where I taped it onto my body, it would come loose.

At dinner one evening I was my usual unbearable self. I told my family, who were more understanding than they needed to be, what was bothering me. "I hate this patch. My body is covered with hair, and no matter where I tape it, it comes loose." My daughter, who had had enough of my complaining, said, "Why don't you tape it on top of your head?"

What a terrible thing to say to her bald father. She may be allowed out of her room sometime in 1992.

In each of these three stories (and I don't mean to imply that I've only done three dumb things in my lifetime—I may have done as many as six), I lost my sense of humor. In each of these tales, I not only acted foolishly, but also inefficiently.

Had I sensed the humor in these situations, I would have remained calm. Had I remained calm, I would have reacted more rationally, with more logic. Had I reacted more logically, I would not have done the dumb things that I did.

A sense of humor affects our decision-making mechanism; that's one of the reasons why it's important for business people.

These stories I've confessed to didn't cost me that much. Perhaps some embarrassment and a $150 repair bill. In the business world, though, actions like mine could be terribly expensive, both in actual costs and in harm to one's career.

Humor and logic are closely aligned—probably more closely than we realize. I remember I was shocked many years ago when I first began to write for Phyllis Diller. Phyllis, as you know, does many bizarre, zany, outlandish, crazy lines about herself, her children, her husband, and whatever. Yet, I sent her one joke that was illogical. She sent it back to me with a note reading, "Honey, if it ain't true, don't send it to me."

We can exaggerate a premise, distort it, view it from an oblique perspective; but basically the humor must be true.

Good logic, and consequently sound decisions, must also be based in fact. As our Abraham Lincoln story (page 15) points out, you can draw wrong conclusions from valid facts. Correct conclusions must be founded in truth.

What's the connection between humor and logic? I feel that a sense of humor has three prerequisites:

1. the ability to *see* the facts as they really are.
2. the ability to *recognize* the facts as they really are.
3. the ability to *accept* the facts as they really are.

We seem to lose our sense of humor when any one of these prerequisites is missing. We forget to laugh at ourselves when we're confused—either we don't know what's going on, or we don't know why it's going on. Or sometimes we just wish it weren't going on. We refuse to accept it and wish it would go away, happen to someone else, or happen next week when we'll have more time to cope with it.

Let's look back at my three stories at the start of this chapter. In the first, I didn't even realize there was a problem. I didn't know I was going to the wrong airport. I could have known; it was written clearly on my ticket. I just assumed I would leave from the same airport that I arrived at.

If I had known that the airport was only ten minutes from the hotel, there would have been no reason to get upset with my hosts. They had planned both my arrival and departure adequately. They were perfectly right in realizing that it would be unwise to pay an expensive fee for a limousine that only had to go a few miles down the road. I probably could have walked to the airport and arrived in time. There was no problem.

But, I didn't know the facts. I didn't see the real situation, and I caused myself a lot of unnecessary trouble.

In the second instance, I had the facts. I knew the mouthpiece was stuck and had to be unstuck. But I didn't recognize—and didn't bother to find out—that the problem was easily correctable. My anger blinded my reason and I transformed a minor annoyance into an expensive calamity.

I didn't recognize the reality of the situation.

In the third story I just refused to accept the facts. I knew I had a problem that needed treatment; I just didn't want to admit it to myself. I didn't want to give in to this discomfort without causing some discomfort back. I chose to be a grouch so that I wouldn't be the only person suffering unfairly. Everyone around me would suffer unfairly, too.

The condition didn't warrant this much self-pity. Clear thinking would have shown that all of us will have problems from time to time.

It was now my turn. The medical solution was not a simple or easy one, but neither was it the melodramatic event that I was making it.

I lost my sense of humor about myself and refused to accept the facts that were.

In each case, what I did was dumb. You see, there's another angle to this idea of seeing, recognizing, and accepting the *real* facts. When we do, they are generally less disastrous than the unreal facts.

When we reject the real facts, we have to create new ones to replace them. Usually, we manufacture situations that are much worse. I created a scheduling problem that didn't exist. I battered a petty problem into a $150 repair bill. I worried an ordinary operation into a life or death fantasy. My sense of humor was turned away and replaced with fantasized, manufactured, non-existent problems.

Let me off the hook for awhile and imagine a situation that you may have experienced and see how forgetting your sense of humor can cloud your commonsense reactions.

You're driving along a freeway at a safe, comfortable rate of speed. That's probably about five to ten miles above the speed limit. You have a pleasant station on the radio and you're making good time.

Suddenly, a speeding car swerves into the lane in front of you. He didn't force you off the road or anything. He simply was going very fast and cut ahead of you.

Now you're angry. I mean really angry. You don't even hear the soothing melody on the FM station. You don't care that you haven't been delayed at all. You're still on time for your meeting. All you care about is that this guy insulted you. He demeaned your driving. He implied that you weren't going fast enough for him. He as much as said that you were driving like a sissy.

Consequently, you have only one option. You have to speed up, chase this automobile, cut him off, and prove to him that he should never again challenge your driving skills.

So you do.

You lose your sense of humor. You abandon logic. You react irrationally and chase this anonymous driver, risking your own life and the lives of others on the road in your reckless pursuit.

I know that story is not too contrived, because it has happened to most of us. It has happened to me often.

Let's study how a sense of humor—a sense of logic—seeing, recognizing, and accepting the real facts would have helped.

If you had seen the facts as they are, you would have known that this was a reckless driver. At least, it was someone who drove with more abandon than you're comfortable with. There are plenty of drivers like that on the roads. Some reports say that almost half of the drivers you pass on the highways are under the influence of something—either alcohol, drugs, or common, ordinary impatience.

Rather than being surprised and angered at this encounter, you might have been prepared for it. If you saw the facts clearly, you might have driven, for your own safety, as if all the drivers who share the freeways with you are reckless.

Then you might have recognized that this was not personal. This person didn't cut in front of you to show that you weren't half the driver he was. He didn't want to belittle you. He simply wanted to get where he was going—perhaps faster than he should. He really wasn't interested in tossing down the gauntlet and challenging you to a "drive off."

Even if he were, so what? Your self-worth doesn't depend on outdriving every nut with a driver's license.

And you might have recognized rather easily—with just a moment of reflection—that you wouldn't want to risk your life and property for a clown who will turn off at some exit, never to be seen by you again.

Finally, you would accept the fact that these erratic drivers will always be with us. They'll exist regardless of new laws, stricter regulations, more careful surveillance, and whatever lessons you and I might teach them.

Your life would be calmer and safer if you just permitted them to drive on out of your life.

Let me cite another example of how a sense of humor generated sound logic:

In 1973, I was on the phone with Bob Hope the day his home, then under construction in Palm Springs, caught fire. At first, neither one of us realized how serious it was. He got a call on a second line and said, "There's a problem at the house. I'll call you back."

Before he called back I learned from news reports that the entire roof had burned. It was a costly and serious fire, although, thankfully no one was injured.

When Bob Hope called back he said, "Did you hear about the house?" I told him I had. He said, "Do some jokes about it."

I did the jokes. I wrote things like:

"It's a terrible feeling to wake up one morning and find out the black cloud hanging over Los Angeles used to be your home in Palm Springs."

"I think the fire was caused by a mix-up with the builders. I definitely ordered the place medium rare."

"Everything was fried to a crisp except the water bed. That was boiled."

"Of course, a huge crowd gathered. My house doesn't work without an audience."

"In front of all those people my house was destroyed. Now it knows how I felt in vaudeville."

But Hope's reaction puzzled me. Faced with a setback like this I would have been angry or depressed. Maybe I would have moped around searching for sympathy, or I might have gotten vicious and attacked the builders or the fire department or just kicked my dog. Who knows?

So I asked Hope, "How can you joke about this? How can you take it so calmly?"

His answer was enlightening. He said, "It went up awfully fast. I'm glad it happened now rather than after we moved in."

Because he reacted with a sense of humor—he reacts to almost everything with a magnificent sense of humor—his analysis was perfectly logical.

Those attributes that comprise a sense of humor are the same ones that enable an executive to make sound business decisions. You have to be able to see the problem, analyze it to find the cause, and then, perhaps most difficult of all, be able to accept the problem and its consequences.

As an example, suppose one of your new sales representatives is just not meeting his or her quotas. That's a problem for you as a manager. However, it's a bigger problem if you don't see it. That's why all good executives have a reporting system—a measuring unit—so they can see potential problems developing.

Okay, suppose you see that this new sales rep is well below quota. What do you do? Fire that employee? Well, maybe, but wouldn't it be wise first to find out why the sales are so low? It might not be the salesperson's fault. It may be your fault. Maybe the documentation you released is offensive in this particular region of the country. Maybe one of the plants that used to buy most of the product has shut down or relocated. It could be that the last salespeople, knowing they would be leaving the region, sold at a heavy discount rate in order to sop up all of the profits beforehand. The new sales rep can't sell in an area that's been saturated.

Whatever the reason, a good executive needs to investigate before making a decision.

Then you have to be realistic enough to accept your own findings. If it is your documentation, you have to change it. If it's the sales rep, you have to make that move. You can't wish either one were better than it really is.

Let me offer one final example of this theory of seeing, recognizing, and accepting. The medical problem that I talked about earlier was a cardio-vascular problem that required heart surgery. My cardiologist told me that I was lucky. For many people, their first symptom is their last. They don't survive a first heart attack. I asked why that was. He told me there were three reasons:

First, some of them don't get any warning symptoms. There is no pain, no pressure, no discomfort of any kind. They simply don't see that they have a problem.

Second, many people experience a shoulder or chest pain, but misread it. They assign it to too much tennis, or too much snow shoveling, or any number of other reasons. They feel the symptom, but they don't recognize it.

Third, some have the symptoms and immediately know that they're serious. They know it's their heart warning them of trouble. Yet, they don't accept it. They say, "I'm too young to have a heart attack," or "It'll go away if I watch my diet," or "I'm strong enough to endure this for a while," or "I'll check with my doctor later when I'm not so busy at work."

Unless they see, recognize, and accept the symptoms, they make a very costly bad judgment.

A sense of humor is a sense of reality. It's knowing and accepting the truth. Both good humor and good judgment are based on reality—on truth.

A good use of humor makes you a more effective businessman,

which in turn improves your self-image, which in turn improves your sense of humor. It's the opposite of a vicious cycle!

You can get this cycle going merely by appreciating the power and the benefits of humor in your everyday life, and especially in your business. Learn to lean on it when you need it the most—that is, when you have problems.

That sense of humor clears your mind. It leaves it free to appreciate the true facts. That vision permits you to make logical judgments. There are more benefits of humor in the workplace. How can we overlook them?

Will Rogers' comments usually were as philosophical as they were funny. (Have you noticed how often, in talking about humorists, the words "wit" and "wisdom" are linked together? That's what this chapter is about.) I'd like to paraphrase one of his lines in summing up business judgment. "A committee was formed to study the high cost of doing business. They turned in their report which said, 'We find the cost of operating our business very high and we recommend more funds to carry on the investigation.'"

CHAPTER SIX

Humor Is Not Necessarily Jokes

A friend of mine has a promiscuous sense of humor. He not only laughs readily at practically anything, but he laughs loudly and vigorously. I would like to multiply him one thousand-fold and take him on all my speaking engagements as my personal audience.

Despite that glorious, hair-triggered laugh, I rarely tell him a joke. Why? Because I'm dreadfully afraid that he'll try to tell me a joke in return.

Then his infectious laugh becomes a turncoat. It switches from friend to foe. He giggles and guffaws so much throughout the telling of the story that it not only becomes three times as long, but also unintelligible. You don't hear words; you hear random syllables interspersed through giggling.

He can take a delightful joke and make the retelling of it just slightly less painful than root canal work.

Bob Murphey, a popular and delightful humorist, once told an audience of speakers, "The first thing I look for in any room that I speak in are the 'exit' signs." He continued, "I'm not afraid of fire. I've been a volunteer fireman in my town for many years and I have a healthy respect for fire, but I don't fear it. I'm not afraid of a major catastrophe. Most hotels are prepared for that sort of thing and a minimum of common sense ordinarily will rule the day. So I'm not afraid of catastrophe. What I am deathly afraid of is the guy who grabs me by the lapel, gets right up close to my nose, and says, 'Have you heard that one about . . .'"

There *are* people who can't tell a joke. Every time I speak to speakers about humor I hear the complaints. "I try to tell jokes, but nobody laughs," "Everybody recommends opening with a joke, but when I do it ruins the rest of my talk," "I can't tell a joke." Then they tell me a joke and I believe them.

People like this shouldn't tell jokes (at least, not yet. The condition is real, but not always incurable.), but they can still use humor.

The point is that humor doesn't always imply jokes, stories, or anecdotes. Wit is not limited to those stories that begin with "These two guys went into a bar . . ." Humor is an attitude; it's a style; it's a flair.

Not all funny people, even professional funny people, are joke tellers. Bob Hope is not a storyteller. He does do jokes, but they're one-liners. He rarely tells an anecdote, a story-type of joke. Myron Cohen, on the other hand, was a professional comedian who told nothing but stories. Cohen would come on stage and proceed from one anecdote to the next without even a segue. With his Jewish dialect Cohen would tell about a woman who went into the corner grocery store. "How much a pound for the lamb chops?" she'd ask. The butcher said, "$1.45 a pound." She'd say, "$1.45 a pound? Across the street I can get lamb chops for $1.20 a pound." The butcher says, "So why don't you buy them across the street?" She says, "They're all out of lamb chops." He says, "When I'm all out, they're only 98 cents a pound."

Cohen would tell his story well, but with no frills. The joke stood or fell on its own merits. Flip Wilson would tell jokes, but he would add to them. A little story like the one I just quoted might become a 10-minute routine for Flip Wilson.

Bill Cosby never tells a story in his nightclub routine. He rarely does a one-liner. He makes observations that we all recognize as true—and funny.

There are as many different styles of humor as there are humorists. There can be as many different styles of humor in business as there are business speakers. Don't limit yourself to jokes or stories. If the professionals did that, you might never have heard of Bob Hope or Bill Cosby. You certainly never would have heard of Marcel Marceau.

It may be heretical for me, a comedy writer, to say this, but comedy is not material. It's not jokes, stories, business—none of these. These may be a part of the humor, but the real key to being funny is characterization. It's the attitude.

Let me redeem myself with my fellow writers by elaborating on this point. Most of the comedy writing that I do lately is for Bob Hope. Forgive my ego, but I write very well for Hope. I've been doing it for almost two decades now, so I must be doing something right.

I also speak to businesses, associations, clubs, and just about anyone who will hire a speaker. My talk is humorous, but I can't borrow any of the material that I do for Mr. Hope. Why? It's not a legal or ethical question of borrowing back material that I've already sold. No, I mean that most of the material is written expressly for Bob Hope. It's designed for his style of delivery and his form of comedy. It doesn't work for me.

But isn't funny material funny material? Not necessarily. I've written comedy material for almost 30 years, and I've never written anything funny. It's not funny until it's put into context or until someone breathes life into it.

The stage directions, "She makes a funny face," aren't amusing until Carol Burnett looks at Harvey Korman and raises one eyebrow. The audience now laughs. It's now funny. Then Carol takes that as a cue to change the expression. The audience laughs louder. Now Carol abandons the funny face for just a second and throws Harvey another look. Now the audience is hysterical, and the words, "She makes a funny face," have described something hilarious.

All professional comedians have a unique style that they've developed and the material must fit them exactly. Good, solid, well-crafted comedy material means nothing unless it complements that unique style. That's why my colleagues and I can write material that earns Bob Hope giant laughs, yet won't get any raves for an aspiring young comedian. Why? Because he or she hasn't yet found that comedic voice. We, as writers, don't yet know who we're writing for. We know what Bob Hope is expected to say. We know how Johnny Carson might comment on a particular topic. We feel we can put words into Phyllis Diller's mouth. But we don't know this young comic. Neither does the audience. For us to offer funny words, he or she must develop a funny style.

Let me take this one step further with a hypothetical example. Let's suppose that I'm treating all of my readers to a night on the town. Hypothetical or not, let's limit ourselves to a two drink maximum. We're going out to see two comedians, let's say, Robin Williams and

Bill Cosby. Now both of these gentlemen are polished performers. Each one has exceptional comedy material.

However, before we begin our jaunt, I'm going to take Robin Williams' script and deliver it to Bill Cosby. I want him to perform Robin's stuff tonight. And I'll give Cosby's material to Williams. Do you expect to see two virtuoso performances this evening? No. Why not? The performers are still superior. The material is unchanged. Why doesn't it work?

The comedians are not themselves. They're not working with their own characterizations. They're dealing with a totally different style. They're just not going to be funny.

What does all this philosophical discussion about the comedy styles of professional entertainers have to do with the business speaker? Two things:

> 1) You need to develop a distinctive, yet natural style of humor. More correctly, you need to rediscover the style you already have, and use that rather than someone else's style.
>
> 2) You need to select your material carefully so that it complements your style.

Let's talk about the first point. You've never thought much about a style of humor. You're not interested in a distinctive comedy persona. You're a business person; not a fledgling comic. Why do you have to concern yourself with this style?

Actually, this is more important for your work than it is for the professionals. They do comedy for comedy's sake. If they get laughs, they're successful. You may get giant laughs from your audience, yet be a flop as a communicator. A touch of humor is simply a device to transmit your message. That's all it should be.

A professional comic can be zany, bizarre, wacky. Your humor has to be natural, organic. It must flow from your personality. Anything less might diminish your professionalism.

Let's take another look at professional performers. Some comedians have tremendous staying power. Others arrive, shine brilliantly, and disappear. Why do some, like George Burns, remain popular for a lifetime while others, like Vaughan Meader (the guy who used to do the John Kennedy impression), fade from the show business scene?

I have a theory: the comics who last are the ones that you would like to take home to dinner with your family. That's the test I apply to young comics to see if they have a chance of a long professional life.

What I'm really checking out is whether their humor appears natural. You can imagine how pleasant it would be to have George Burns at your dinner table. First of all, he's a celebrity. That's always exciting, to be rubbing elbows with the great. Secondly, George is fun. He's witty, he's bright. He'd be a delight to talk with. Vaughan Meader was a celebrity, too. He'd be someone special to invite to a family dinner, but if all he did was talk in the John Kennedy voice, you'd grow weary. You'd ask an interesting question and get a Kennedy-like response. Eventually, you'd have to say, "Mr. Meader, be yourself. It's all right. We'd like to get to know you."

I don't mean to imply that Vaughan Meader wouldn't be an interesting dinner guest. What I do mean is that his comedy style wouldn't be. When there is constant tension between the real person and the stage persona, we become uncomfortable. That's why I feel those performers will eventually disappear from the scene, while the more natural ones will continue.

Let me explain one other thing, too. The professional stage comedy of these "natural" comedians is well prepared. It's written with devotion and rehearsed diligently. It doesn't just happen. But the style *appears* natural—that's the secret. I was tempted in that last sentence to say "relaxed." But that would be wrong because "natural" doesn't always mean "relaxed." George Burns is certainly relaxed, but Woody Allen is a funny, nervous wreck. But that's natural because that's Woody. Woody Allen is uptight, so his comedy should be.

Any style that is affected is wrong for you, the business speaker. It may be funny; it may be hilarious. That's great for you as a comedian, but it's not desirable for you as a communicator.

People want to feel comfortable with you at the podium. They want to like and trust you. If your wit is too different from your own personality, it causes a tension, maybe a distrust.

You need to be yourself. We know how much we respect that in candidates that we interview for employment. If they're honest, sincere, and candid, we tend to accept a few of their flaws. If they're pretending to be something that they're obviously not, we wonder what's wrong with that personality they're hiding from us. Audiences, too, wonder about you when you're not totally honest with them—even in doing humor.

Do you enjoy telling stories when you're out with friends or family? Then tell them to your co-workers, your clients, your employees—whoever your audience is. Do it naturally and they'll buy it from you. If you don't enjoy stories or don't tell them well, don't put them in your speech.

Do you use street lingo normally? Then use it in your comedy. If you converse in one-syllable words on the job, don't use four-syllable words in your story telling.

I remember once when a sports writer did a story about a high-school basketball player from our neighborhood. The writer attributed a very controversial statement to the youngster. I asked another friend who played on the same basketball team if this kid really meant what he said. My friend said, "He don't know if he meant it or not. Three of the words in the statement he don't know the meaning of."

Do you speak with literary jargon naturally? Then use it in your wit. W.C. Fields was a comic who loved the multi-syllabic. From him, these stilted sentences sounded typical:

> "I always keep a supply of stimulant handy in case I see a snake, which I also keep handy."

> "What contemptible scoundrel stole the cork from my lunch?"

Notice, it's not "whiskey" or "booze;" it's "stimulant." That's funnier from W.C. Fields, for some reason. He also would call a thief a "contemptible scoundrel" instead of a "jerk."

A good example of different styles, especially in the use of words, was Bob Hope and Bing Crosby in the road pictures. Crosby was an admitted word-lover. He played them the way a jazz artist plays his instrument. I've heard Crosby ask not for a drink but for "a bit of the bubbly." Hope would go for the simple word that made the joke crystal clear, while Crosby would go for the melodic, grandiloquent term that he could almost sing rather than speak. Both were funny, but each was different.

The best style to develop is the one you already have. Capitalize on your own personality because it's the one that requires the least work. It's also the one you've been doing the longest and the one your acquaintances know best. Also it reflects your preferences.

Study yourself and honestly assess your personality. Don't say you don't have one, because even that is a distinctive style. I emceed a retirement banquet for a fellow worker who was a quiet, lackluster gentleman. He wasn't happy with his forced retirement at age 65. We all got nervous when he began his farewell speech at his party because we feared it might be a lament that would kill the festivities.

He said, "What can I do now that I'm leaving my place of employment? Where can I be wanted now that I'm no longer wanted here?" "Oh, boy, this is going to be real fun," we all thought. He went right on. "When racehorses can no longer run, they're retired to stud." His eyes brightened up with that and he said, "Hey! Now there's an idea."

It got laughter and applause.

Now let's talk about the second point, the selection of material. Once a speaker or a performer discovers that comedy voice, it dictates the material that person should use.

As I mentioned earlier, it's easier for a writer to write for Bob Hope or Johnny Carson than for an unknown, though promising, comedian. All of us know what Hope or Carson might say, so we writers compose something that is consistent with that. None of us knows yet what the unknown might say, so it's harder to focus the writing.

There was a great joke in radio years ago. Jack Benny, the quintessential cheapskate, was accosted by a mugger. "Your money or your life," the crook threatened. There was no reply. After a beat, the audience broke into loud laughter. Only Jack Benny would have to ponder that.

The hood repeated his threat, "Your money or your life." Jack Benny said, "I'm thinking it over." The audience roared.

It was the perfect gag for Jack Benny. If Bob Hope's character was asked, "Your money or your life," he might have replied, "I take it you're from the IRS."

"Your money or your life" posed to Johnny Carson might have gotten the reply: "Haven't I been married to you?"

Even comics who are very similar in style have material that is individualized. A writer friend of mine recently had a newspaper article written about her career. The piece listed several one-liners that she had written for various clients. She asked me what I thought after reading it. "I enjoyed it," I said, "but I think the jokes you did for Phyllis Diller should have been sent to Joan Rivers and vice versa." She said, "That's where I did send them. The reporter mixed them up in the story."

When you select or write your material, first consider the form of the humor. Should you use anecdotes, one-liners, simple asides, or quotes from other people? Or should you use all of these in some combination?

You use only those that complement your characterization—your comedy persona. Actually, I shouldn't call it your comedy persona; I should call it your speaking persona. Your material should complement your professional speaking technique.

Decide what you are going to do based on your ability. Can you tell a story? Then tell one. Can you deliver a good one-liner? Then do it. If you can't; don't.

Part of the form, also, is the language you use. Is it literary, conversational, or street lingo? Use whatever gets the point across, provided you're comfortable with it.

When I visit comedy clubs around the country I hear some good material laced with obscenities. Often the vulgar language is not part of the joke; it's there only for emphasis or color. I'm not comfortable speaking in public that way, so I would change that material. If cleaning it up destroyed the comedy, I wouldn't use that humor.

However, I sometimes throw a "hell" or "damn" into my presentation for the same reason. In my opinion, it gives the joke more impact. Some people aren't comfortable with these invectives. Then they shouldn't use them.

The material you select must represent you—your talents, your style, and your beliefs.

You also have to judge the content of your material. You must know what it says and be certain that it says what you want to say. Many well-known comics have been criticized for controversial comments. Afterwards, some of them said, "I had no idea the joke meant that." They didn't mean to offend, they just didn't realize what they were saying. They knew, of course, that the joke was funny, but they didn't look beyond that. As a business communicator, you'd better look.

Also, make sure the humor you're using makes the point you're trying to make. Remember, you're trying to get a message across. You're trying to convey that message more effectively with a touch of humor. You defeat your purpose if the humor conveys the wrong idea.

We've used Abraham Lincoln as our model raconteur. If the accounts in the books are right, he was. His stories illustrate his points very clearly. They are not all hilarious, but they are all enlightening. That's what he wanted. Presumably, it's what all business speakers want.

However, not every one of us has to have the collection of anecdotes that Lincoln amassed. Nor do we have to have a book of jokes always open on our desk. There are as many different styles of humor as there are humorous speakers. With some experimentation and analysis, you'll find the one that works for you. If you're happy with it, the audience usually will be, too.

CHAPTER SEVEN

But I'm Not a Funny Person

Some people complain not only that they can't tell a joke, but that they're not funny. That I don't believe. Everyone can get laughs. Test me. Next time you go to the airport, observe. Eighty percent of the people are fun to watch. They bring chuckles without even trying. That's in the general corridors of any terminal. Go into the VIP rooms, and the percentage rises to ninety percent. How hilarious could those people be if they worked at it?

Don't tell me you've never gotten laughs. I travel around the country and try to be funny at banquets and seminars. Some of my biggest laugh getters, though, have been on the planes travelling to make my speeches. One time I tried to coax some recalcitrant salad dressing out of its tiny plastic container. I coaxed it so well that it blew up in my face. The flight attendants were very attentive and helpful. They also worked quickly: they wanted to get out of my sight so they could laugh their silly heads off.

I avoided this problem on my next flight by upgrading to first class where the salad dressing is served in civilized containers. So are the drinks. I ordered gin on the rocks, which they presented to me in a comfortable, heavy, real-glass glass. I enjoyed one sip and then dropped glass and contents square on my crotch. Pain struck my consciousness first, followed closely by unbearable chills. Embarrassment chased both of these when I realized that I needed assistance—quick. If you want to see how easily you can get laughs try walking down the interminable, narrow aisle of a stretch DC-9—from seat 1C to the service station at the end of the plane—with a wet stain decorating the front of your trousers.

You know you can confess to equally awkward blunders that produced chuckles—maybe not to your face, but behind your back or hidden behind the open pages of magazines. People have laughed at you somewhere. The trick now is to get them to do it on purpose.

I can hear you arguing with this logic in your head. "Sure, everybody does something dumb in their life. We all look stupid from time to time. That's different from getting laughs from the platform." Sure it is, but my point is that you can't classify yourself as a person who can't get laughs. You can, you have, and you will.

As an experiment when I lectured before a regional meeting of Toastmasters International, I asked for volunteers—people sitting in the audience who felt they couldn't get laughs. Many hands shot up. I invited a few of them to come on stage to see if they could get laughs with my help. Three timidly agreed.

I didn't plant these volunteers, nor did I prepare anything with them ahead of time. I had never met them before (I hadn't even known if I would be able to get anyone to volunteer that night).

I had prepared material. I gave each volunteer a copy of his or her script and asked them to study it for a few minutes as I continued with the lecture. Later, they came back onstage to read the dialogue.

One of the volunteers, a soft-spoken woman, took over the lectern and the microphone at my invitation. She was to read a joke that I had guaranteed would produce laughter. She read only a few sentences when I interrupted with some pointers. Her stance wasn't powerful enough. She straightened up and I stepped aside, as she continued. I stopped her again to recommend that she speak with more conviction. She nodded obediently, and went on. I interrupted once more to suggest more effective line readings for her. She nodded approval and continued again. Once more I stepped forward. She quickly turned to me and said, "Will you leave me the hell alone?"

The audience screamed. They loved it. She had stood up to authority. She put this pompous, interrupting ass in his place. What the audience might or might not have known—it really didn't matter—was that her outburst was written into the script. The joke she was reading was irrelevant. It was the set up for this—her put down of me—that was the joke.

The woman who swore she couldn't be funny got big laughs. What's interesting, though, is that the woman enjoyed her new-found skill. Throughout the rest of the lecture, whenever I called on her or she came onstage, she played that same character—the performer who had put the coach in his place.

Each of the other two experiments worked as well. It wasn't that these people couldn't get laughs; it was that they believed in their unfunniness so firmly, that they never tried. They surrendered before the battle began.

An interesting event in my life puzzled me then and puzzles me now. I stood in line to see Phyllis Diller appear on *The Mike Douglas Show* when it was broadcast from Philadelphia. Phyllis asked me to see the performance and then meet with her in the dressing room afterward.

As my wife and I waited in line outside the studio, a young fellow came up to me and said, "Are you Gene Perret?" I said I was. He said, "Come on up to Miss Diller's dressing room. Phyllis has to leave immediately after the show, so she would like to meet with you now."

I met briefly with Phyllis and then went down to sit in the audience for the telecast. As we walked back to the studio I asked the young fellow what made him come right over to me in line. We had never met before. He hesitated to answer for fear that I might get angry. I assured him I wouldn't, and he said, "Phyllis Diller told me to go to the line and find the guy who looked the least like a comedy writer." He picked me first.

Phyllis was doing a joke and his selecting me was coincidence, I'm sure. (At least, I hope I'm sure.)

What does a comedy writer look like? Dick Cavett doesn't look much like Woody Allen, but they're both comedy writers. Some of my colleagues look like fallen-away football players, others like accountants. A few look like international terrorists. We don't fit into a mold that you can classify as "comedy writer."

You can't judge a book by its cover; you can't predict how funny a person will be by their looks. Some, admittedly, you might look at and say, "I hope that person is a comedian because he's never going to make it as anything else." Nevertheless, appearance doesn't determine funniness. Bob Newhart looks as normal as any one of us, but he's funny. Jerry Lewis doesn't look too normal, but he's funny.

Personality, dress, manner of speech, voice volume, facial expressions, gestures—none of these makes you funny. Neither do they rule out your being funny. Look at some of the professional comedians.

Bob Hope and Johnny Carson have a quiet, dignified wit; Buddy Hackett has a boisterous, Brooklyn kind of comedy. Alan King screams his jokes at the audience; George Burns has an unassuming, almost reluctant, humor. Comics can be loud, like Jackie Gleason; they can be timid, like Jackie Gleason's "poor soul." Funny people can be sloppy, careless, and carefree like Oscar Madison in *The Odd Couple*; they can be finicky, straightlaced, and meticulous like Felix Unger.

Humorists can speak out of the side of their mouth, like Buddy Hackett. They can speak with a heavy dialect, like Jackie Mason. They can have a resonant, disc-jockey voice like Dick Cavett. They can whine, like Roseanne Barr. They can stutter. We have a writer on the Bob Hope team who makes jokes of his stuttering. He told me once to give him a call at home. He said, "I-I-If n-no one answers, d-d-don't hang up. Th-th-that's me."

Comics can be strong and athletic, like Bob Uecker, or they can even be physically handicapped. A very good writer in Hollywood who has muscular dystrophy began his career as a nightclub performer. He kidded his handicap. He would say, "I can drive a car, you know, but it's difficult. My automobile insurance costs me $1200 a year—and that's just on the inside."

Any person or personality can channel humor. You can. I know you can.

Humor accepts all applicants. You can't escape because of size, personality, speech patterns, shyness, or a note from your mother saying, "Please excuse Martha from Wit 101 since she is not funny."

Can a big man get laughs? Brad Gilbert, who won the humor competition on *Star Search* is 6'9". Yet Mickey Rooney gets his share of laughs at only 5'2". Oliver Hardy proved that fat men get laughs; Stan Laurel showed that slender men do, too. Phyllis Diller kids her unattractiveness, but Lucille Ball was a showgirl who did all right with comedy. Good-looking men like Johnny Carson can be funny, and the late Marty Feldman got laughs with his unique face.

The list could run for 26 pages if we allowed it. We could give examples of all different sizes, shapes, and personalities. Regardless of what you look like, sound like, or smell like, you can be funny.

The advantage of all this is that you don't have to change anything to add humor to your talk. You needn't become louder, or more animated in your gestures. You don't have to become more outgoing or more belligerent. The way you are right now is perfect. Be yourself, because there is a comedy style to fit you.

Too often we try to be funny with someone else's style or material. You might be doing a Robin Williams routine when you're more like a Bob Newhart personality. You might be trying to be George Burns when you're really closer to Don Rickles. That's pointless. As some wit once said, "It's like trying to teach a pig to sing. It not only wastes your time, but it annoys the hell out of the pig."

You already have a manner, style, and personality that is tailor-made for you—and for your comedy. You may feel it's not right for comedy because it's not like any humor you've seen. That may be true because no one is exactly like you.

The faults that you feel are interfering with your humor are the ones that might trigger your biggest response. Don't try to hide them behind a Borscht Belt comic's demeanor. Let them shine. Let them be funny.

Remember we discussed earlier that humor is truth. If you want to find the humor in any topic, seek it in reality. That same principle holds for developing your comedic personality.

Each of us is a different person. Each of us is composed of strengths and frailties, pluses and minuses. Be honest about your failings. If you're shy, let your audience know that you know you're shy. If you're a "loudmouth," tell the audience that no one knows that better than you. Audiences are sympathetic and understanding. They normally don't hold our minuses against us, provided we own up to them.

How many times have we heard in national scandals that so and so could have been forgiven if only he or she would have admitted the transgression? "Confess your wrongdoing," Joe Q. Public says, "and I can forgive and forget."

Audiences are not only kind to speakers who own up to their shortcomings, but they're appreciative. Each listener knows he or she has weaknesses. They'd like the speaker to be one of them—to admit to failings of his or her own.

In the opening of my banquet speech I tell about my kindergarten-age daughter who asked me to help her with a poem she had to recite at school. I said, "Sure, Honey, Daddy will help you; but you know that Daddy writes for some pretty famous people. Why don't you let me write something extra special, just for you. Then when you give that at school it'll be funny, it'll be different, and it'll be totally yours." She thought about that for a little while; then she said, "Well, Dad, this is going to be in front of the whole school. I'd rather it be good." The story works well because the listeners enjoy a comedy writer putting down his own comedy writing, instead of boasting about it (which most of us do pretty well, too).

Kidding yourself is not a sign of weakness; it's a sign of a strong self-image—that's a plus for an executive. It's telling your listeners that you have so much confidence in your abilities that you can allow them to take a little ribbing, even from yourself.

Here are a few different ways I've heard professional and amateur speakers kid themselves and their weaknesses:

> I spoke at an awards banquet where a former member of the host association returned for a visit. He was 90 years old. He knew they were going to invite him to say a few words, so he rehearsed a little routine with me before the banquet. I agreed, and here's how we presented the joke to the members.
>
> As emcee, I spoke with this gentleman when he came to the microphone. I asked him how he was doing and he said he was doing just fine. "In fact," he continued, "I just got this new hearing aid which is fantastic. It's expensive, it's state of the art, and it's the best hearing aid money can buy." I took my cue and asked, "What kind is it?" He glanced at his watch and said, "It's about eleven-thirty."
>
> Bob Hope kids his age with, "People ask if you can still enjoy sex over 70. Certainly you can, but it's safer to pull over to the side of the road."
>
> And, "I enjoy sex as much at this age as I ever did—especially the one in spring."

One Toastmaster admitted to being nervous about having to deliver his first humorous talk. He also kidded himself about being short. He said, "I was so nervous about giving this humorous talk that I hardly slept at all. I was up the entire night pacing back and forth under my bed. . . ."

Another speaker at this same Toastmaster meeting kidded his less-than-dynamic personality. He said, "I told my wife that I was worried about this humorous presentation. I said, 'I can't figure out anything to talk about that will get laughs.' She said, 'Just tell them about our honeymoon.'"

Another woman speaker at that affair confessed to her frustration over the humorous speech. She said, "I asked my husband, 'What can I possibly do to get laughs?' He said, 'Enter a beauty contest.'"

Roseanne Barr chides her own performance as a housewife and mother. She says, "When my husband comes home, if the kids are alive, I figure I've done my job."

Phyllis Diller never professed to be a great housewife or cook. She tells about the time "a grease fire broke out in my sink. The firemen arrived and put it out, but three of them had to be treated for food inhalation."

Are you shy? You can't be any more timid than the henpecked husband who said he was "afraid to tell my pregnant wife that I'm sterile."

Some of you may say, "Wait a minute. I don't want to wave my failings before a strange crowd to have them ridiculed." Then don't. That's your decision. Hide them. Cover them. Mask them with make-up. Lie about them, if you want. Don't use them, though, as an excuse to avoid humor.

Humor is very flexible. You can use it to present your idiosyncrasies to an audience, or you can use it to hide those same idiosyncrasies from them. You can use humor as the cathartic that presents your minuses to your audience and begs their indulgence. Or it can be the distraction that camouflages your weakness. It can be a diversion that allows you to escape from an audience with your dignity intact.

If you seriously want to mask a trait, simply manufacture another one and toss it to your listeners. Create something you're not so sensitive about and kid yourself about that. Your audience will bite.

Does any humorist mention anything about Dolly Parton except the obvious? Does Bob Hope razz Gerald Ford about anything except his treacherous golf game? Dean Martin jokes exist today because Dean needed something to build his act around after he split from Jerry Lewis. He decided to become a drunk—a stage drunk.

If you don't want people to kid you about being short, then joke about the way you dress. People will accept it.

I used to write countless flat-chested jokes about Phyllis Diller. "I buy two kinds of bras—plain and mercurochrome," "I put my bra on backwards one day, and it fit," "I have trouble buying brassieres. I take a 32-long." Audiences listen to Phyllis and laugh at these gags even while they're looking at her on stage. She's a well-developed woman.

Probably the greatest example of a mythical defect was Jack Benny as a miser. He was known as the stingiest man in the world because he had his writers, from radio days, paint him that way. He did the jokes on himself, too. He once appeared at a charity golf tournament. After entertaining the gallery at the first tee, the tournament executives insisted that Jack begin play. He turned to his caddy and said, "Are you any good at finding lost golf balls?" The kid said, "Yes, Mr. Benny, I am." Jack said, "Well, find me one and let's get started."

You are you. That's where your humor should begin. Don't bend yourself to fit any material. Bend all material to fit you. Find material, alter material, or write new material that suits you—your personality and your style. You're more important than any piece of material.

As a professional writer, the first thing I have to know with any assignment is who I'm writing for. I have to watch the client perform. I have to see and hear the comedian. That's the only way I can write material that is going to suit that person.

"Suit" may be the proper word because it's like going to a custom tailor. The tailor can't produce a suit until he or she measures you. Likewise, all comedy should be custom-made.

You have a unique managerial style. As an executive you're one of a kind. You follow general precepts, but you follow them your way. You have an individual communication style, too. All of this—

everything that makes you "you"—goes into building your peculiar style of humor.

Begin building your humor from within so that it complements your unique individuality. Don't abandon who and what you are to be a humorous somebody else. Be yourself and enjoy it!

PART II

Creating Your Humor

"There is no good reason why a joke should not be appreciated more than once. Imagine how little good music there would be if, for example, a conductor refused to play Beethoven's Fifth Symphony on the ground that his audience might have heard it before."

A. P. Herbert

CHAPTER EIGHT

Okay—How Do I Go About Giving Humor a Try?

The first part of this book admittedly has been sermonizing. I've been trying to convince you that humor is an effective ally of the business speaker. I've been trying to persuade you to try it as a communication tool.

Now we need to get down to the nuts and bolts of using humor. If I've convinced you to try a dash of wit, then I owe you a step-by-step procedure for introducing some light-heartedness into your speaking. Let's get to it.

How do you go about giving humor a try? Gradually. You add humor to your talks bit by bit as you would salt to a recipe. Too much can ruin the soup. Two rules of thumb will be stated or implied throughout this book: First, in dealing with humor, less is more. Shakespeare said it well with "Brevity is the soul of wit." Second, if in doubt, cut it.

Professional comics are careful always to "leave 'em laughing." They're anxious to leave the stage with their listeners still wanting more. They don't want their comedy to wear out its welcome. With a touch too little humor, you create a longing for more. With too much you bore your audience, destroying whatever good your humor has accomplished.

Being forewarned (and you'll be warned many times more), you can now begin to give humor a try. To do that sincerely you have to commit to the effort and make the effort.

Commit to using humor. Despite all my proselytizing and cajoling in Part One, I'm sure there are many people who are still fearful of using humor in public. That's normal. They say that many great comedians are frightened before every show. They are not sure the audience will appreciate them this time. Being afraid shows that you have a healthy respect for humor, which you should have. However, to give it a fair try and to honestly evaluate the results, you need to approach this experiment at full throttle. If you don't, you'll fail.

Writers and performers don't always agree on what's funny. The writer can argue, stomp his foot and bang his fists, maybe even convince the performer to try the line at rehearsal; but he can't win the argument. Why? Because when the performer says the line in question, he or she says it without conviction. The performer may not "take a dive" intentionally, but it doesn't matter. Without an energetic reading, the line is lifeless. It has no chance for survival. The performer says, "There I tried it and it stank."

You can't fold like that and get an honest appraisal. If you're going to try this experiment, give it everything you've got (in small, bite-sized bursts, remembering our warning at the top of this chapter). Be honest with yourself, and don't make just a half-hearted effort. That will profit you nothing except the right to say, "I told you so."

There's another reason for attempting humor with all-out enthusiasm. That reason is survival. So far in this text, we've painted a rosy picture of comedy. It is delightful, but it has a dangerous side, too. When you try it and fail, it's painful. Professionals have a graphic description of the anguish of a bad audience reception. It's called "Flop-sweat." They also call it "dying." Professionals are not real fond of the experience. You won't be either.

Some trial runs you can approach with a lackadaisical attitude because you're not in jeopardy; someone else is. For instance, if your boss wants all reports typed on 16-pound paper instead of 20-pound, you don't care. You still get paid for writing them. If the higher executives are offended, it's the boss's tail that's on the line, not yours.

That dispassionate stance won't wash under all circumstances, though. You wouldn't use it in bullfighting, for example. You can't get into the ring with a fierce animal and say, "Aw, I don't care if I do this well or not." If you're going to commit to getting into the ring with this angry beefsteak, you'd better commit to some expertise, too. If you wave the red flag half-heartedly, you're going to wind up standing for the entire plane ride home—unless you know how to sit comfortably with a horn embedded in your bottom.

"Anything that's worth doing, is worth doing well." That bromide applies particularly to humor.

Apply some effort to your humor. Comedy is deceptive. When it's done well, it looks easy. When it looks the easiest, is when the most effort has gone into it. Bob Hope kids, "I don't need my writers—unless I want to ad-lib something." It's his way of showing some appreciation for us, but it also makes the point that even his offhand remarks are carefully thought out and prepared.

As a beginning comedy writer, I had the opportunity of seeing Sammy Davis do his nightclub act twice a night for two weeks. Writers were as anonymous then as they are today, so I could mingle with the crowd after the show and overhear some of the comments. People would say, "Boy, that Sammy Davis can ad-lib, can't he?" "He has a clever comeback for everything." What they didn't realize was that most of those comebacks were ad-libbed the same way, with the same inflection, at the same point in the show almost every night.

I'm not implying that Bob Hope and Sammy Davis can't think on their feet or can't come up with clever, genuine ad-libs. I've been around both of them many times and they are bright and funny. What I am saying is that they are consummate professionals who know that not too much of a stage presentation can be left to chance. The bulk of it has to be written and rehearsed before the curtain goes up.

Lots of work goes into a nice, easy piece of comedy. It has to be conceived. That may take the most effort—coming up with the original idea. Then it has to be written, and rewritten, and rewritten again. For every funny line that you hear in a movie, on TV, or in a club, countless other funny lines have been tried and discarded. Then the line has to be rehearsed. The inflection and timing have to be perfected. After all that effort, the line may hit or miss. Then the process goes back to square one and begins again.

You're not exempt from this effort because you're non-professional. You can't sidestep the work because this is just an experiment, an attempt at humor. No, you have to work harder because you don't have the experience to lean on.

I was once with Sammy Davis in Florida when he agreed to make an appearance at a benefit show. The producer was delighted that this big star agreed to appear, but he was also nervous. He kept asking, "What will you do? Do you have music? Won't you need time to rehearse? Will you sing or dance or just talk to the crowd?" Finally, Sammy got slightly annoyed at this man's fidgetiness, and said, "Look, man, after 60 years in the business, just bring me out. I'll think of something."

He did, too. He broke 'em up. You and I couldn't do that. We'd have to put in untold hours of preparation. Sammy had put in 60 years of preparation. There's no way to avoid doing the work.

You have to work at:
1) Finding or creating your style
2) Gathering your material
3) Adapting your material
4) Delivering your humor
5) Working your humor into your presentation

What sort of work do you have to do?

1. Finding or creating your comedy style: My friend, Vic Braden, says that any novice who picks up a tennis racket will do almost everything wrong. What feels normal is almost always incorrect in tennis. That's probably true in humor, also, except with a confusing twist: What feels natural in comedy is to try to act unnatural. Insecurity probably prompts most people to imitate someone else. They feel their normal speech and gestures aren't funny enough, so they borrow someone else's. The logic is, "It got laughs for her, so it should get laughs for me." It got laughs for her because it was natural for her. What will get laughs for you is your own style.

Many young comics learn their trade at local comedy clubs nowadays. That's good. It is a training ground that wasn't available years ago. There's a drawback to it, though. They all begin to sound alike. I can't imitate the style, and I surely can't do it in a book, but if you listen to beginning comics, you'll hear the same speech patterns over and over again. Each punchline is emphasized the same way. Often there's no punchline there, just the speech rhythm.

I want to grab some of the younger comics in a paternal stranglehold and say, "Be yourself. Use your own speech patterns." The material would not only be different, but it would be funnier.

So you have to work at two things. Well, maybe you have to work at the same thing from two different angles. First, avoid hiding behind someone else's technique. Second, struggle to find and feel comfortable with your own style.

How do you do this? Often, awareness is the answer. Don't allow yourself to do anything too differently with your humorous material than you would with any other material. Become sensitive to when you're being yourself and when you're being phoney.

2. Gathering your material: We've already learned that humor isn't jokes and stories. It isn't the material. However, material is an aspect of comedy that can't be overlooked. Funny stuff doesn't make a humorist, but you can't have a humorist without it.

There are many places to find usable material, as we'll see in Chapter 11, and gathering material is easiest when you make it an ongoing process. Collect and assemble material you like, so it will be available when you need it. That's better than doing the research at the last minute, when you absolutely must find something that fits in this particular spot in your speech.

However, you do have to know what you're looking for. Obviously, you want material that's funny. Or do you? I heard a story once about the late Colonel Sanders of Kentucky Fried Chicken fame. He was on an airplane, and a young infant was screaming loudly and incessantly. Nothing would quiet the youngster. The mother and the flight attendants tried all their tricks to no avail.

Finally, the Colonel asked if he could hold the baby. He picked it up, cradled and rocked it, and the child soon went peacefully to sleep.

When he returned to his seat, a nearby passenger graciously thanked him. "We all appreciate what you did for us."

The Colonel said, "I didn't do it for us. I did it for the baby."

That tale is not a big laugh-getter, but it's a delightful piece of material. It's got a touch of humor, some pathos, and a lovely message. It might be worth snipping out and putting in your collection.

You want to *understand* any material you collect. As a young scamp in high school, I once played a trick on the class nerd. We didn't call them that in those days, but you get the picture. I concocted some joke that made absolutely no sense, but I had several of my friends in on the gag. When I told the "joke," they would all roar uncontrollably. The fun was watching the nerd's reaction. Naturally, he laughed. Then we laughed all the louder at his laughing.

The amazing thing was that all the nerds we tried this on repeated the joke to other people. They couldn't have understood the punchline because there was no punchline, but they told it anyway. Don't do that.

Make sure you understand any story you repeat. Know why it's funny, or at least why it's worth retelling.

Once you understand it, be certain it's a tale you want to tell. I used to tell a joke that I wrote years ago. I don't tell it anymore. Why? Because it's an unfair joke. It's a gratuitous shot at certain people, and I don't want to take that shot anymore.

I'll quote the joke, but purely for academic study.

> "I saw a twelve car pile-up on the Expressway today. What happened was a woman signalled for a left-hand turn and eleven drivers believed her."

I still think technically that's a good, well constructed joke. I just don't want to say it. It's not only because of the feminist movement, although that probably heightened my awareness. It's that it's unfair and untrue. Women are not bad drivers. My wife says the worst are old men who wear hats, but that's her prejudice. She'll have to write her own jokes.

3. Adapting your material: Rarely will you find a chunk of comedy that you can retell as is. A joke or a story is a naked thing. It has no relation to you, to your audience, or to your message. You have to work to make it personal.

First you ask, "How can I make this story mine?" One way is to translate it into your lingo. If the original story says "Mother and Father," you might feel more comfortable saying "Mom and Pop." Don't tell the story the way you heard or read it; say it the way it should sound coming from you.

I once wrote a television sitcom in which I repeatedly used the word "Grandmom." The producers had the entire script retyped substituting the word, "Grandma." It didn't make that much difference, but I was curious so I questioned it. They told me that there was no such word as "Grandmom"—nobody used it.

Obviously, I used it. But they were correct. They all felt uncomfortable using a word they were unfamiliar with. It didn't trip out of their mouths easily, so they changed it.

You also have to work to localize your story, make it apply more to you or to your audience. You accomplish this by extracting the essence of a story and then changing or rearranging the accidentals.

Does a story that is told of two astronauts in a spaceship work just as well when it's you and your carpool buddies on the way to the office? If you have a story about shepherds, does it stay funny if you tell it about welders?

Each change depends on the story and you and your audience, but you get the gist. Rather than tell a story about some strangers on the page of some magazine, it's usually better to relate a tale that applies to this group assembled before you.

4. Delivering your humor: You have to tell this story or joke that you've researched, so you must make sure that it's a story you *can* tell. That's not always possible. When I first began writing, I worked with a black comedian. He had some stories that were priceless, but I couldn't retell them to friends. He told them in his natural speech pattern, which was a black dialect. That dialect was necessary to the joke. When I tried to tell it without that, the comedy disappeared. When I tried to tell it with the dialect, I either did it badly, or it appeared in bad taste.

Not all of us can tell every joke. Some jokes require a boisterous reading, and some raconteurs are too genteel to yell like that. Just as some vocalists perform better on ballads and others shine on up-tempo tunes, so some people tell one type of joke better than another. Test each story you're going to tell; practice it if necessary; but be sure you *can* tell it.

Tell the tale in your natural speech, using your natural inflections. Usually phony accentuation doesn't help a story except to emphasize perhaps that the story needs help.

Practice the story several times—on yourself and on others. Say it aloud, in front of a mirror, if you wish, until you're convinced that you can tell it well. Try it on friends.

5. Working your humor into your presentation: How you get into your funny story is important. "I'm now going to tell you the funniest, greatest, most hilarious joke you ever heard in your entire life." Use that preamble and you'd better have the funniest, greatest, most hilarious joke these people have ever heard in their entire lives, or your joke is going to have a hard time.

You'll have to put some thought and effort into your transitions. It's always nice to have them fit naturally into your presentation so that the joke sort of slides into your talk unannounced. It sneaks up on the audience that way.

The following analogy works well to explain this concept of transition. I liken a joke, or more specifically a punchline, to pulling a rug out from under unsuspecting victims. You have to position them properly on the rug. That means you, as the story teller, have to lead them where you want them. You have to direct their minds in the direction you want them to go. Then you have to tug on the rug at the precise moment. If you do it too early, they're not on the rug yet—you've accomplished nothing. If you let them know you're going to do it, they'll step off and again—no result.

In effect, you have to outsmart your audience. That takes effort and preparation.

Let me give an example of the sort of work you need to do to make your humor effective. Recently I heard a joke that I mentally filed away for future use. I heard it this way:

> "A guy was driving with another guy and he went right through a red light. The first guy said, 'Why'd you do that?' The driver said, 'My brother taught me to drive. He always does that.' Then they came to a stop sign and the guy went through it again. The other guy said, 'You did it again.' The driver said, 'Yeah, I know. My brother always does that.' They came to another red light and the guy went through it again. Same reason—'My brother always does it.' Then they came to a green light. The driver stopped. The guy said, 'Why'd you stop for the green light?' The driver said, 'My brother might be coming.'"

I enjoyed the reverse logic of that story.

Not too long ago I spoke to a group of pharmacists. During my research, I learned that one of their pet peeves was doctors who insisted on handing out drugs. These professionals felt that doctors shouldn't dispense medication; pharmacists should.

Early in my speech, I mentioned that I had visited my doctor and told him that I would be speaking to an association of pharmacists. Then I got into the joke this way:

"My doctor said, 'Oh, I got a great joke that the pharmacists will love. You know, I know pharmacists and I know they'll love this joke.'"

Then I told the story, pretty much the way it's written above. It got a nice laugh, but I ended with:

"Now I told that story for only one reason. To prove that I agree with you people. I don't think doctors should be allowed to dispense humor, either."

I found a joke that I liked and understood (as much as anyone can understand the wackiness of that joke, but I did know why it was funny), so I filed it away. Then I changed it slightly, so that it fit into this presentation. I did force the telling of it a bit, but that was because I wanted it to appear awkward so that I could get in that last line about dispensing humor.

It became an effective piece of humor that applied to this particular audience.

As a way of convincing yourself that you can do humor and that it will be effective for you, collect some material. Research or recall some funny stories or jokes.

This collection process will tell you something about your sense of humor. You may begin to see a pattern in the type of gags that you collect. I have a friend who loves cartoon humor. In his speeches, he illustrates each of his main points with a cartoon. He describes the drawing and then narrates the caption. It's surprisingly effective.

When you've assembled a reasonable amount of copy, select one story for your initial experiment. Now translate it. Convert it from whatever language it's in presently to *your* language. Make it sound like you.

Find a reason for telling it. Does it illustrate a belief of yours? Does it apply to someone at work—or whatever? Make it apropos.

Then practice telling it. Make sure you can say all the words, and say them with conviction. Try it out on friends and a few small groups.

Hear the laughs and where they come in the story.

If the process was successful, you have one piece of humor in your arsenal. If it wasn't successful, find out why. Experiment with new inflections, new words, new gestures in the telling of the story. Try to convert it to a success. If that's impossible, pick a new anecdote and start the procedure from scratch.

All you want is one success to start the process.

Once you're successful the first time, you can do it again, and again, and again. Each time you do it, it becomes easier. Eventually, you'll build up a dependable repertoire and you'll be honing the skills that you'll need to add a touch of humor to any speech.

CHAPTER NINE

How Much Humor Should I Use?

I've gotten into the habit of sprinkling red pepper on every pasta dish I eat. I don't taste it first; I just sprinkle. You know the kind of pepper I mean—those little dried flakes of dynamite that come in a sprinkle type jar. I like the hot, zesty flavor that it adds to the meal.

To me, this seasoning adds interest to the dish. You've probably gathered by now that I feel the same about humor and communication. A dash of it helps.

It would be ridiculous, no—suicidal—for me to swamp my pasta with red pepper. As much as I enjoy the tangy taste of the condiment, I enjoy the flavor of the pasta more. I just want some spice to augment the meal; I don't want to blow my brains out with the first mouthful. A surprise taste treat in every third or fourth forkful of macaroni is enough; I don't want to be gasping for breath and gulping down water throughout dinner.

That's how much comedy you should use. For a business speech, comparative measurements should be about the same. And for the same reasons.

My palate considers red pepper a good thing; I consider humor a good thing. It is. A brisk walk in the morning is also a good thing for your well-being, but not if you walk from Wichita to Pittsburgh. Piling on more of a good thing doesn't make a better thing.

Remember your reason for stepping to the podium in the first place. You have a message to convey. That message should remain central, the focal point of your discourse. You use humor to augment it, not overpower it.

Some singers have asked me, as a humor writer, to work on their nightclub act. They wanted it spiced up with some comedy. At our meetings they often ask, "What should I do at this point in my act?" My answer usually is, "Sing."

People don't pay good money to see Frank Sinatra in concert doing an impression of Jerry Lewis. I'm not implying that Mr. Sinatra is one of my clients, but if he were, I'd tell him that, too. "Do more singing than joke telling." A little humorous patter serves a purpose in a vocalist's act. It allows the audience to get to know him better, it gives him a chance to rest between songs, and it promotes a good atmosphere in the audience.

You're not a vocalist. At least, I hope you don't sing your speech to your employees or customers. If you do, you need more help than this book offers—and so do your listeners. No, you're a business speaker, but, like the vocalist, you need to limit yourself to a little bit of entertaining patter.

Here again are the axioms that I promised would repeat throughout this book. "Less is more," and "If in doubt, cut." Picture the red pepper again. Sprinkle too little on the pasta and you haven't done much harm. Shake out too much and you may have to throw the meal away.

Wit generates respect for the speaker. Someone once said of humility, "Once you think you've got it, you've lost it." In other words, it's impossible to be proud of your humility. Respect is similar in that the harder you try to get it, the more difficult it becomes to achieve.

People tend to offer their respect to those who aren't seeking it. Once they notice that you're actively pursuing their respect, they withhold it.

A former musician told me about a hot, new drummer who came on the scene. Several musicians went to hear him play in a club and they were quite impressed. He was good—damn good. At the first intermission, he visited the musicians at their table. The whole time he was there, he told them what a great drummer he was. He wanted to make sure that they heard all his great riffs. He desperately wanted them to admire his skills.

My friend said, "When he got back on the bandstand for the second set, his left hand wasn't that great."

Obviously, he was as accomplished a musician for the second half of the evening as he was for the first. He had overdone it, though. He became so arrogant that they began to inspect his technique more closely. He had tossed away the respect he had won.

That can happen on the platform. You win some respect with a pleasant story, then you try for more and more of the same. The audience catches on and says, "Wait a minute. Let's take a closer look at how he's using that left hand."

Aside from the arrogance factor, too much comedy can destroy the respect you earn simply by exposing your poor judgment. A pleasant, incisive, funny story wins an audience to your side. They like you for it; they respect you. Then overdo it—throw too much red pepper on the pasta—and they re-evaluate you. They say, in so many words, "Anyone who mis-measures one ingredient by this much can't be trusted with other decisions."

Obviously, the turnaround will not be so dramatic. They won't throw bouquets on stage at one minute, and toss tomatoes the next. It's a subtle reaction. It's those subtleties, though, that add up to an audience's reception of your message.

Another purpose of your humor is to get people to listen. However, once you get them listening you have to tell them something. If you tell them another two or three jokes, you're going to lose them again. Remember the entertaining flight attendant who opened this book? She told us a one-liner that perked up our ears, then she immediately told us where the exits on this airline were. She got our attention and she got her message across. You have to strike while the iron is hot.

People can be receptive when they're in a congenial mood. A prison psychologist, John Deery, knew that. He was selected by the authorities to go into the prison library and talk to rioting inmates who had commandeered that building. The prisoners were armed, angry, and out of control. Deery had to surrender himself to them and try to convince them to end the uprising.

Armed guards surrounded the library from a cautious distance. Everyone was tense as John Deery began the somber walk toward the prisoners' stronghold.

As he walked, he began to feel like a gunfighter facing his rival in a western gun duel. All eyes, prisoners' and officials', were staring at him. He began to swagger. As he got more into his fantasy, picturing himself as Gary Cooper in *High Noon*, he began singing that picture's theme song loudly. "Do not forsake me, oh my darling, on this our wedding day-ay."

The prisoners were dumbfounded. The prison officials glanced at one another in bewilderment. "Do you think we sent the wrong guy?" they silently wondered.

Deery continued to stride and sing. The prisoners, the guards, the officials all began to laugh at this man's antics. His behavior was ludicrous in such a serious, tense situation. It was funny.

The prisoners welcomed him in. They talked, and he convinced them to surrender. Was Deery wise, wacky, or damned lucky? Regardless, consider what his fate might have been if instead of beginning the talks when his ploy got everyone laughing, he said instead, "Wait a minute. If you liked that, wait till you see my impression of Donald Duck, then I'll follow that with my impersonation of Jimmy Cagney trying to sell a vacuum cleaner to Katherine Hepburn."

Timing is often promoted as the essence of humor. It may be, but part of good timing is knowing when to stop using humor, too.

Another purpose of humor is to help your listeners remember your main points. To accomplish that, your humor should be graphic and simple. If it isn't simple, it is confusing.

In Chapter Two, we tried a memory experiment. It was admittedly long, but it had to be to challenge your recall. How difficult was it to remember just two or three numbers? Yet, each segment was simple. The text offered just one image for each two-digit portion of the number. If you performed the test, you'll remember how effective it was. You might be able to recall even now many or all of those numbers and their sequence.

However, if the text had offered three or four different examples to choose from, instead of just one, you would have been confused. It would have been much harder to recall which image applied to which number. Rather than making the recall easier, it would have made it almost impossible.

In offering light entertainment as an aid to memory in your speech, keep your examples simple: Less is more.

Entertainment—comedy—also serves as refreshment for a weary audience. As good an orator as you may be and as captivating as your topic is, your listeners still tire. It's work to listen to an interesting speaker. It's more work for the audience than for the speaker. You *know* what you're talking about. You've thought it through beforehand. The audience has to hear, listen, analyze, and evaluate. They also have to separate the wheat from the chaff. They're not going to accept totally everything you offer. That entire process is mentally fatiguing.

A snippet of comedy is your reward for the effort the audience is exerting. An entertaining aside is a recess in the middle of your speech. Try not to make it "Spring Break."

Perhaps this chapter hasn't really answered the title question, "How much humor should I use?" We've only offered cautions against overuse. It's difficult to give a quantitative answer because each situation is different. Each reader has to make his or her own "seat of the pants" judgment, but I can suggest a trial and error system to help you find the appropriate measure.

You need to discover your own ratio for humor to message. You mix it the same way you mix cement or batter for cookies. Start with the basic ingredient (in this case, your message) and then add humor—gradually—stirring all the while. As you're adding and stirring, keep evaluating. If the mixture's too dry, add more liquid. If the batter's too runny, add more powder. The key is to blend gradually, evaluating the result constantly. If the end product looks good, try a touch more and taste it again. Perhaps you overdid it with that last bit. Remove it and add it elsewhere, or cut it and try a different bit of humor. Stir that into your mixture and taste again. It has to be a trial and error process. Proceed gradually and cautiously.

How will you know if the results are good? You will, that's all. One of the advantages (and at times, disadvantages) of humor is that you get instant feedback. The audience is honest. Even when they try to disguise their response, they'll be honest. Nothing is more obvious than polite laughter. Now you have to be honest in evaluating their response to your material. If it's working, pat yourself on the back. If it isn't, try to make it work or drop it and try something new.

One final caution. Humor is heady stuff. It's addictive. Be aware of that and remember that the message is your mission at the platform. Stop when you have added enough humor, no matter how tempting it may be to add more.

Less is more. When in doubt, cut.

CHAPTER TEN

Where Do the Jokes Go?

There was this lady who had a chance at winning the big money in the lottery. She won the money and immediately called her husband and said, "Start packing. I won $10 million." Her husband said, "That's great. But wait . . . should I pack summer or winter clothes?" She said, "I don't care. Just be out of the house by morning."

Why did I start a chapter with that joke? I have no idea. It's a fine joke, but does it really belong here at the beginning of Chapter 10? Not really. It could just as easily have been the start of Chapter Six or maybe even Chapter 17.

I do know why I started this chapter with it, though. I wanted to show you that you don't have to start with a joke. It's a myth that's been repeated by many speakers, but it's not true. It's another sign of the fear of using humor. A speaker feels humor should be in the speech somewhere, so he or she puts it at the beginning—to get it over with.

No, you're not obliged to begin with a laugh. Neither are you forbidden to.

Some of my favorite one-liners come at the start of a talk. Johnny Carson began his TV monologue on February 9, 1971 with a great opening joke. Of course, the straight line registered 6.5 on the Richter Scale. At about 6:01 that morning, Los Angeles was rocked with a devastating earthquake. Carson came onstage that evening and said, "The God is Dead meeting that was scheduled for tonight has been cancelled."

I wrote an opener for Bob Hope that I'm proud of. It was for the televised celebration of his 80th birthday party from Washington D.C. Mr. Hope sat in the Presidential Box with Ronald Reagan while other entertainers—Phyllis Diller, Ann Jillian, Paul Anka, and many others—entertained them for almost three hours. Toward the end of the festivities, Bob Hope came onstage to give a short thank-you monologue.

He told the writers, "We have to say something about sitting there with the President." I came up with this line for his opening:

"You gotta know what a thrill it is for me to sit in the Presidential Box with the President of the United States, Ronald Reagan. You know, when we first walked in, there were only two chairs in there. One was marked 'Number One American,' the other was marked 'Washed Up Actor.'" After a timing pause, Mr. Hope went on. "Boy," he said, "did we fight over those."

Someone once wisely observed that you don't get a second chance to make a first impression. You also don't get two shots at an opening joke. That joke should be chosen carefully. It sets the tone not only for the rest of your humor, but for the rest of your speech.

Not all jokes have to have a point. They don't all have to say something to your audience. That's an old-wives' tale (or an old-speakers' tale—to be more accurate and less sexist). The point of some humor can simply be, "Let's have fun. You've been a good audience and you deserve a laugh." We'll talk about those jokes in a while. An opening story, though, should have a point.

We mentioned earlier that there is some tension when an unknown speaker approaches the podium. There's also some confusion. They don't know why you're there, if you're any good, if they should listen to you, or (if it's a concurrent session) whether they selected the right room.

Opening with a pointless story—a joke for a joke's sake, because some "old-speaker" advised you to always open with a joke—will only confuse them more.

There are times when that may be what you want—to confuse for the moment in order to make a point forcefully. That confusion naturally creates tension in the listeners' minds. When you resolve that tension, you hammer an item home. In an earlier example, Knute Rockne used that ploy when he didn't show up for his halftime tirade. Remember? He just popped in and said, "Excuse me. I was looking for the Notre Dame football team."

I once heard a gentleman deliver a very dynamic talk to a group of speakers on "Professionalism." He began by apologizing. "I don't have a speech prepared for this session. I honestly tried to write on this subject, but I have nothing to say." Then he explained that while he was struggling to compose a speech, his wife kept offering unusable suggestions. "Talk about how those speakers should learn to finish their talks on time. They're supposed to be so damned professional, yet they always run late. I could write you a half-hour speech on that myself." Then this gentleman explained that he couldn't use a half-hour speech because he was only allowed 30 minutes for his remarks. "Since the previous speaker will probably run about 10 minutes too long," he explained, "I just won't have time for that long a talk."

In claiming to have no prepared speech, and in giving the reasons why none of his wife's suggestions worked, he got our attention and delivered a useful discourse that taught us quite a bit about being professional.

Any opening humor should apply to your audience and be apropos. I sometimes make my opening apply directly to the audience. For instance, "It's nice to be here with all you insurance people. It's easy to tell this is an insurance agents' convention. I stopped a man in the lobby and said, 'How do I get to the main ballroom?' He said, 'You go right down this hallway, then turn right. You can't miss it, but God forbid if anything should happen to you, how's the little woman going to get there?'"

The same formula applies to other professions. I don't mean to pick on the insurance folks. "It's easy to tell this is a management convention. I stopped a woman in the lobby and said, 'How do I get to the main ballroom?' She immediately appointed a committee to get back to me in three months with an answer."

The opening story can also apply to you. Recently a breakfast club made up entirely of CEO's in one city, invited me back as their speaker. I worked in a story that I had heard about repeat performances. It went:

"It's nice to be back with you gentlemen. It's always a compliment for a speaker to be invited back, but it's also a challenge. It's like the politician of many years ago who was campaigning for re-election. He visited one town and was delighted. He was lucky enough to visit on the day they were having a public hanging. Everybody turned out for that so he could reach all the voters with just one talk. He asked the mayor if it would be all right if he addressed the crowd. The mayor said it wouldn't bother him if it was all right with the hangee. The man said,

'It's okay with me if he says a few words, but could you hang me first? I've already heard him speak.'"

The best opening humor also encapsulates the occasion. It's a precursor of what's to come, a light-hearted preamble. Politicians often open with humor because it gives them that common touch. They arrive in a limousine with bodyguards. They get a reserved parking space, which most of us would kill for. Then they try to appear just like you and me. (Humor usually does it for them, too.)

But they're very good at epitomizing their speech with the opening few sentences. I just saw Richard Gephardt's withdrawal speech from the 1988 presidential campaign. He said (and this is not an exact quote), "They say the opera isn't over until the fat lady sings. Well, after our defeat in Michigan the other night, I distinctly saw her approaching the microphone."

It's cute, light-hearted, a chuckle-getter, and it tells you exactly what's coming next. You know that he's going to end his candidacy.

Opening humor is not mandatory. If you do use it, though, make sure it does open your speech. It shouldn't be a device that postpones the opening of your speech. That's what many jokes become when they're thrown in to fulfill that "opening humor" requirement. Speakers say in effect, "Let me tell this joke and get it out of the way, and then I'll get on to my speech." Don't do that.

Now let's discuss three different methods of positioning the humor in your presentation. They are:

1) Spaced regularly throughout

2) Positioned to clarify or reinforce your salient points

3) Positioned to refresh or reward the audience

1. Spaced regularly throughout your presentation: This is probably the neatest and most clinical arrangement. It's designed like a boxing match. Your audience gets so many minutes of combat time followed by a brief respite. I don't mean to imply that listening to your speech is like getting pelted about the face and body by an angry opponent, but you get the picture.

You analyze your speech, find places that are relatively evenly spaced, and insert humor. The value of this system is that it keeps your audience alert. There's a little reward for them every so often. They come to expect it and pay attention to the important parts in between the jokes, too.

Some television writers follow this precept in scripting sitcoms. One producer advised his writers to underline all the punchlines in their script. He wanted to see no less than three red lines per page. To him, that guaranteed that the audience would stay amused and not wander to another channel.

You might wonder with a system like that, though, if it didn't get in the way of the dramatic moments. Strangely enough, that's when jokes are needed most and get the biggest response.

I remember one episode on the sitcom *Soap*, when the Billy Crystal character was confessing his homosexuality to his aunt. It was a touching, dramatic moment. Defending his lifestyle to her, he named several famous homosexual men in history. "Oscar Wilde, Michelangelo, Plato. . . ." That stunned her. She looked at her nephew with sadness in her eyes and said, "Mickey Mouse's dog was gay?"

The Mary Tyler Moore Show, *All in the Family*, and many other shows would always take the edge off those serious moments with some fun. Playwrights have done it for years. It's called comedy relief.

The same logic applies to speaking, too. The heavier your message gets, the more passionate you tend to get about it. It's a serious point you're making and you present it fervently. There's a danger hidden in your enthusiasm, though. You can get so caught up in your message that you become a cartoon, an unbelievable fanatic. You become so narrow-minded about that one point that you drift away from the reality of things, at least in the eyes of your audience.

The harder you work to be believed, the more skeptical your audience may become. That's why we sometimes laugh at the more flamboyant television evangelists.

Wit brings you back down to earth. You may still be as passionate about your idea, but you show your listeners that you've put it in perspective. You become a real, in-touch, flesh and blood person, and your message becomes more acceptable.

In using this method of spacing humor, the material doesn't necessarily have to apply to your talk. It can, and is probably better if it does, but there's nothing wrong with just taking a short break and throwing in a quote, anecdote, or joke that you feel your listeners might enjoy. That's because your primary purpose in sprinkling humor throughout is to keep your audience alert, to keep them listening. If it does that, whether it applies or not, it has served its purpose.

2. Positioned to clarify or reinforce your salient points: Remember what Lincoln said about telling stories? "I do not seek applause . . . nor to amuse the people. I want to convince them." When he wanted to make a point forcefully, he made it with a story.

Positioning your humor by this method is like strengthening your writing with modifiers. Consider these sentences:

"The man gulped his drink."

That sentence is grammatically correct and conveys information.

"The thirsty man gulped his drink voraciously."

This sentence tells us more and paints a more graphic picture. We know why the man is gulping, now. He's thirsty. The guy in the first sentence could simply have been a slob. The adjective clarifies the sentence.

We also see in this second sentence how the man is drinking. He's attacking the liquid. We know what gulping is, but the adverb explains the action more fully.

Adjectives and adverbs, though, must be used carefully if they're to be used correctly. A writing instructor once pointed out to me that not all adjectives and adverbs modify. Some of them do nothing. They just sit there. He said, "Calling a mountain 'majestic' doesn't tell the reader much about it. All mountains are 'majestic.'" But a "hot" drink is much different from a "cold" drink. Those adjectives qualify the noun "drink." They tell us something and serve a purpose. The same principle should apply to adverbs.

More importantly, the same applies to humor that you would position to clarify or explain your main points. It should be appropriate to the point you're making and should say something about it.

Lincoln would have convinced no one if his stories were confusing. They had to be very explicit in explaining his thoughts. This following example would apply as much today as it did in Lincoln's time:

Lincoln was trying to fire up some of his campaign workers, when a few of them tried to quiet his fears by telling him that rumors about Ohio preferring Salmon P. Chase for President "all amounted to nothing." Lincoln answered, "That reminds me of a story. Some years ago two Irishmen landed in this country, and, on a walk in the woods after work, came suddenly near a pond of water. To their great horror they heard some bull-frogs singing their usual song—croak, croak, croak. They listened and trembled, and feeling the necessity of bravery they clutched their shillelaghs and crept cautiously forward, straining their eyes in every direction to catch a glimpse of the enemy, but he was not to be found. At last a happy idea came to the most forward one and he sprang to his mate, and exclaimed, 'and sure, Jamie, it is my opinion it's nothing but a noise.'"

Perhaps Lincoln went on after that anecdote, but did he have to? Didn't that story chide the offenders effectively enough?

Generally, when you try to clarify a point, it's wise to place an appropriate piece of humor before it—the same way an adjective usually goes before the noun it modifies. The humor you present contains the essence of your thought, as Lincoln's tale did; then you can expand on it later.

I once heard a CEO address his top executives. One of the programs that he had introduced during the year was a foolhardy flop. They all knew it, and to his credit, he did, too. More importantly, perhaps, he was willing to take the blame. He began with a story:

"I once saw a man park his car in a clearly marked 'no parking' zone. Two policemen came by and one tried to politely warn him. 'I wouldn't park there,' the policeman advised. The guy was too arrogant to take any advice. 'It's a free country, man. I can park anywhere I damn well please.' The cop warned, 'If you park there, I'll have to give you a ticket.' The guy wouldn't listen and the exchanges went back and forth for a minute or two. Then the other cop said, 'Let me try.' He approached the driver and said calmly, 'This is a no parking area and I want you to move the car right now.' 'Says who?' the guy asked. 'Says me and my billy club,' the cop replied, and then bopped him right on the head with his nightstick. The man got in his car and moved it to a legal parking space. Now the first cop was puzzled. He said, 'I tried to ask you nicely. Why wouldn't you move the car for me?' The man said, 'You didn't explain it to me like he did.'"

The CEO continued, "Gentlemen, this year we've had the realities of this business explained to us. We got the message."

The man's entire speech was contained in those opening few minutes. He admitted the flop, that it was largely his doing, that it was a mistake, but that both he and the company had learned from it. Now they were going to attack the future.

The rest of the talk, at least the part about this point, was amplification.

When you want to reinforce, or help your audience remember an item, it's wise to put the humor *after* that item. That's similar to the adverb that follows the verb. You present your proposition in your oratory, then hammer it home with some humor.

Again, whatever illustration you select should be apropos and clear.

I once heard a manager warning his employees that all evaluations for the coming year would be based on performance. "Not on the way you dress," he said. "Not on how nice a guy you are. On performance."

Then he followed that with a story "about a pitcher for the Mets who felt he was underpaid. The pitcher was a graduate of Yale. He complained to his manager, Casey Stengel, 'Do you realize I'm the lowest-paid member of the Yale class of 1959?' Stengel said, 'Yes, but you've also got the highest earned-run average.'"

Probably not too many of the listeners forgot that their salary rewards would be based on results.

3. Positioned to refresh or reward the audience: Regardless of how masterful an orator you are, you're audience is going to tire. You're giving them solid information that they must digest. You've got their minds working. You've got them thinking, analyzing, dissecting. You're working the hell out of them. Give them a break, will ya?

Literally, they need a break, a small recess. They need to let their minds stop working and to relax and chuckle for a beat or two.

Professional seminar leaders often give their listeners physical exercises to refresh them. It's exhausting to just sit for a long period of time. So they interrupt their talk and have the audience stand and stretch, or walk around—anything to get them off their butts.

I attended one seminar where the speaker asked all of us to go around the room, silently, and look deeply into the eyes of as many people as we could. She asked us to remember what we saw there. This naturally got us out of our seats and walking around the room, exercising our weary bodies, and doing a little giggling, too. It's not easy to stare into some stranger's eyes with a straight face. Then she told us that if we noticed anyone's pupils dilating as we gazed at them, that signified that person was sexually attracted to us.

We all laughed and ad-libbed our own jokes about that comment. There was probably no scientific basis to the observation, but it was a pleasant break from just sitting and listening.

Your "recess," of course, doesn't have to be that big (remember this was an all-day seminar). You may just need a short quote, a clever aside, a joke, or an anecdote. In some cases, just a glance or a gesture is enough humor to get the job done.

Where do you put these little breaks? Anywhere in your talk where you feel they're needed. If you were listening to what you're saying, when would you want to take a small, mental break?

It's up to you to decide when you've worked your audience enough. When you have, reward them.

This humor doesn't have to apply to your talk. It doesn't have to emphasize or reinforce any of your topics. It simply has to be fun, enjoyable, and relaxing.

If you're using your humor as a listener's reward, you may want to announce it. Tell them you're getting away from the serious stuff for a minute. Invite them to rest and rejuvenate their minds along with you. If you use that device, without over-using it, the audience feels like they're getting a bonus, something thrown in for nothing.

This is as simple as saying, "We'll get back to this in a minute, but first I gotta tell you what happened the other day. . . ." And tell them.

Sometimes if I'm giving a seminar, I'll break and ask some of the attendees to tell me a joke. I get some interesting stories that way, and have a lot of fun. People surprise you.

I might even follow with this anecdote:

"I sometimes talk about creative writing to the grammar school youngsters in my community. I used to ask them to tell me a joke, but I had to stop. You're never quite sure what they're going to tell you. I got scared once when I asked for jokes. One youngster stood up and said, 'Do you know why we have belly buttons?' I answered, 'No,' but I was half afraid to. I thought I might get a bad-taste reply. The youngster said, 'Because when you're up in heaven, right before you're born, God comes along and pokes you in the belly saying, You're done, you're done, you're done. . . .'"

What you want to accomplish with your talk will dictate which of these three methods for positioning humor you'll want to employ.

They're not strict, etched-in-stone rules. They're just guidelines. Trial and error will help you refine the location of the humor in your communication.

Now you're ready for your big finish. Should it be a boffo joke (Boffo is show-biz lingo for a big, solid laugh-getter)? Should you finish with a heart-wrenching, tear-jerking anecdote? Maybe even a hard-hitting threat? How about just a simple "Thank you and good night?"

It can be practically any of those and maybe one that hasn't been thought of yet. Whatever you choose, though, it should be a "button." Button is another show business term that simply means that the ending should feel like an ending. When I wrote for *The Carol Burnett Show*, endings were always a nuisance. Carol would never accept anything that didn't bring the sketch to a proper finale. That's not a complaint about Carol; it's a compliment. She was professional enough, and cared enough about her comedy, not to let us lazy writers sneak in a "this'll do" finish.

You knew when a cowboy movie was over, because the hero always rode off into the sunset. As Pat Buttram put it, "Gene Autry always used to ride off into the sunset; now he owns it."

However you finish, it should be definite. You know a purse is fastened when you hear it click shut. Your audience should hear that "click" at the end of your talk.

It doesn't have to be humor; but if it is, it should be big. Remember it comes at the end, so you have no chance to recover. In the body of your speech, you can always pretend that you didn't want to get a laugh with the joke that just bombed. You can slide by it and get a solid laugh later. Not at the finish you can't. You're exposed. You bomb, and that's it.

As much as I've championed the use of humor throughout this text, I'm not doing it here. I'm not campaigning against it, either. If you do want to end with a joke, be sure it's boffo. Go with a guaranteed, sure-fire laugh-producer.

When you get the laugh, get off the stage.

CHAPTER ELEVEN

Where Do I Get Good Material?

Once I spoke to my neighborhood Rotary club. I won't tell you how much I received for the talk, but if I had given a breakfast speech that morning to another group for $50, I would have averaged $25 per speech for the day.

The club had a visiting Rotarian from India at the luncheon and they exchanged flags with him. At least, they thought they exchanged flags. The visitor discovered that the souvenir banner he had received was from a Rotary club in Mexico.

The embarrassed club president explained that he brought the wrong flag from home. This was one he had received on a visit to Mexico. There were no local pennants available, but the president promised one would be mailed to the visitor within a week or two.

I followed this confusion and began my talk by saying, "I've often wondered why this club doesn't pay their luncheon speakers. I see now that they're trying to save up money to buy a club flag."

It got a big laugh and applause.

That opening joke was practically handed to me. Wouldn't it be nice if all of our humor came that easily? It doesn't. Most of the stories we use require effort and research. Where do we begin this exploration?

Jokes, quotes, and stories like to play a teasing game of hide-and-seek when you need them most. You recall reading a great quote about salesmanship that would be perfect for your upcoming speech, but you can't quite remember what it said, who said it, or where you saw it.

So you begin the hunt. It's not in the book you thought it was in, and you can no longer find the book it might be in.

You call a few friends who have great recall on these matters, but they need more information than you can supply. "It said something about selling is like something else, then ended with a real funny word." "Who said it?" your friends ask. You tell them, "It might have been either George S. Kaufman or Mary, Queen of Scots. Maybe Shirley MacLaine." They hang up.

You don't have time to search any longer for that ideal line you remember seeing (or hearing. That's it. Maybe it wasn't in a book. Maybe you just heard it somewhere. Oh well.), so you look for another piece of humor that will apply.

You find hundreds of jokes and stories about salesmanship, but none of them seems just right. They're all a shade off. Mark Twain once said that the difference between the right word and the almost right word was like the difference between lightning and lightning bug. (See, I did find that quote.) Then someone did a rewrite: "The difference between the right word and the almost right word was like the difference between chicken and chicken pox." (See, I didn't find that quote, so I don't know who said it.)

In using humor, the difference between the perfect story and the compromise is the difference between "funny," and "funny how none of his jokes seemed to work."

When you're desperate for comedy material is the wrong time to look for it. Like a watched pot never boils, the perfect story for tomorrow morning's talk never pops out of a three-and-a-half-inch joke book that's been gathering dust in your bookcase. The search, instead, should be continuous. Devote a few minutes of each day, or at least each week, to the hunt for humor. That way you'll build up a dependable, usable repertoire of applicable material.

"How can it be applicable," you ask, "when I don't even know which speech it will apply to?" That's a good question. So good, in fact, that we'll devote a later chapter to it. For now, though, let's stick to where to look and what you're looking for.

What you're looking for primarily is material that entertains *you*. Do *you* think it's funny? Do *you* feel a piece of material says something? Do *you* think a quote or story gets a message across clearly and forcefully? If a chunk of humor impresses you, then you can use it sometime in the future. Save it and file it.

The reason most jokebooks don't surrender the joke you need

when you need it is because 95 to 99 percent of the material in the book either doesn't apply to you or doesn't hit your funny bone. Yet each time you do research, you have to page through and read over this large percentage of unusable material. It's inefficient.

Every so often, I review an auditioning writer's work with Bob Hope. The comment I hear most frequently from the comedian is, "You have to read through a lot of stuff to get to the good ones." That's a negative. Comedians want to spot a lot of usable material quickly and then select the absolute best. Their time is valuable and so is yours. You want to search and save only the material that you feel is good—usable material.

Don't worry at this point where or how it will apply. Just find stuff that you like.

Where do you look?

1. Your own memory: There are lots of places to hunt for usable humor. The first, and potentially the most productive, doesn't require any page turning. It's your own memory.

I'm not a great joke rememberer—most comedy writers aren't. If we remember too many jokes, we can't clear our brains to write the new jokes that provide our livelihood. When we have to create, that great joke rolling around in our head inhibits us. We keep wanting to write a variation of that one. So we forget jokes quickly.

Yet, gather a few of us together and start a story-telling session, and we'll bring up jokes from years ago.

You've heard, told, and appreciated many jokes over the years. You probably can't recall one off the top of your head, but they're in there somewhere. A concentrated effort can force them to the surface. At least, it can raise many of them.

Allow a few minutes of concentrated time to recall some stories that you've appreciated in the past. Jot them down and put them aside. They might be useful.

Another valuable resource is your family heritage. Most families are similar. We all have a skeleton in the closet that's wearing a red clown's nose. Some aunt or uncle was a little nutty. Mom or Dad said something that should have been reprinted in *Reader's Digest*. I used to do a joke where an interviewer asked me if anyone in my family suffered from insanity. I answered, "No, they all seemed to enjoy it."

At family reunions, my brothers and sisters enjoy telling funny family stories. My wife tires of it because she insists (rightly) that they're always the same stories.

Review your family history. There might possibly be humor there that your audiences would enjoy.

Recall your own history, too. It might yield some valuable material that you've never noticed before or simply forgotten.

When I first came out to Hollywood, I was kidded for dressing more like an engineer than a writer. When I went to work on *Laugh-In*, I thought I'd dress a little more hip. It didn't work. My first day there I wore some "in" shoes. They were silly-looking, but I thought they were "hip." Apparently, they weren't because I took another ribbing. I tried to end the assault with a weak joke of my own. I said, "You can kid me all you want, but these shoes were given to me by my father on his deathbed." A fellow writer answered, "What did he die of? Embarrassment?"

Most of my material comes from this area because I talk about my work in comedy, and because I meet some interesting, glamorous people in show business. Funny things happen, though, in every office, in every profession. With concentrated effort, you'll be able to recall several incidents.

If the stories aren't polished, finished, or perfect for presentation, that's all right. You're just gathering raw material for use later. When you're ready to use them, you can add the finishing touches.

2. Friends' memories: There are two things that people can't keep to themselves—bad news and a funny story. Those of you who travel can verify that the joke you hear boarding the plane in Los Angeles is the same gag you hear when you deplane in Kansas City. When a good joke surfaces, it travels fast because people love to tell a story.

Also, when you tell an anecdote, people want to reciprocate—or retaliate, depending on how good your story was. You tell a joke and someone will want to tell you one. The first comedian I worked for, Slappy White, used to do a joke in his nightclub act about that:

"People ask me where I get these funny jokes. Well, I get them from you people. I go to the bar and you folks tell me stories. I take them backstage, clean them up . . . ."

People do love to tell funny stories. You can take advantage of that and gather material just by listening. No, I take that back. Do more than listen; goad them on. Get them to talk more by asking questions:

"What's the dumbest thing you ever did on the job?"

"Have you ever had a boss you totally disliked? Tell me about him."

"What's the most embarrassing thing you've ever done at work?"

You'll not only get some usable material, but you'll also be appreciated as a good listener.

You can prompt people to tell funny stories, too, by offering one first. Tell your tale, and someone will try to top you. This is the way Lincoln began his joke file as a travelling lawyer.

Can you use this material you glean from others? Sure, if the story doesn't have to name names to be effective. You can change certain incidental elements of the story or shroud your telling of it in anonymity. Or you can politely ask permission. Most people accept this request as a compliment. They're pleased that you liked their anecdote that much. I'll sometimes say, "I love that story. I hope you don't mind if I use it sometime." Generally, they're flattered.

Be wary, though, of stories that are almost a part of our folklore, yet people tell as true. These are apocryphal tales that have circulated for years, usually told as actually happening to "my aunt" or "my sister."

An example? There's the story "that actually happened to my aunt who lives in New York." (That lends it believability.) Her husband came out to go to work one day and there was this note inside their car. It said, "I borrowed your car last evening. I've been out of work for sometime and I needed a job to support my family. The only way I could get to this one job interview was by 'stealing' a car. I got the job, and I appreciate your help. In this envelope are two tickets to the Mets game for Friday evening. They're my way of saying thanks."

They took the tickets, went to the game, and, when they got home, found out their house had been robbed.

That may have been a true story, but it definitely hasn't happened to the "aunt" or "sister" of all the people who tell it. These stories are "public domain" by now, so there's no harm in your using them if they help your speech. However, be careful. If you tell them as true, enough people may have heard them before that telling them makes the rest of your anecdotes suspect.

If you still want to tell a story like this, confess to the audience that it's possibly mythical.

3. Listening to people: Finding humor can sometimes be a matter of putting up your comedy antennae. Listen, because sooner or later somebody will say something dumb, something funny.

How many times have you been sitting at a restaurant when someone comes to your table, points at an empty chair, and asks, "Is anyone sitting in this chair?" Of course, we know what they mean in that instance, but many times we don't. Comedian David Brenner does a whole routine about stupid questions people ask. He ends it with the person who asks David, "Are you reading that paper you're sitting on?" Brenner says, "Yes, I am," then he stands up, turns the page and sits down again.

I heard two funny quotes in one day. My wife and I were flying to Phoenix for a writers' conference. On the plane, I sat in the aisle seat and worked on a final polish of the presentation I was to give. My wife struck up a conversation with the gentleman in the window seat. I didn't eavesdrop; I only heard bits and pieces of their exchange. They were talking about family and the gentleman asked my wife how many children we had. My wife told him, "We have three girls and a boy." He couldn't hear her over the engine noise, so he asked, "Three girls and a what?"

Don't you think he could have taken a wild guess? Three girls and a mushroom. Three girls and a chimpanzee. Once you eliminate girls, there's only one other sex left—isn't there?

Later that day at the conference, a few of us faculty members had a cup of coffee in the hotel restaurant. The lady that worked the counter was delighted to have so many writers and editors as customers. She said, "You people could write a book about working in this place." I said, "Why don't *you* write it?" She said, "Well, I would, but the only thing I don't like about writing is the paper work."

I know that's a famous Peter DeVries line, but I don't think this woman knew it. Unwittingly, she said something witty. I knew that each time we visited this coffee shop, we should pay attention to her comments. They might make a nice chunk of material for later presentations.

I have another friend who specializes in malapropisms. I can't figure out if he does this intentionally or not. If he does, he comes brilliantly close to the cliche, but stays far enough away to be funny. Sometimes his malaprop has more meaning than the hackneyed phrase he's groping for.

I played tennis with him one warm afternoon. As we towelled off between games, he said, "Let's get this game over with. I'm going to have heat castration." Another time he mentioned that his wife was visiting her doctor because of a "virginal itch."

People have said funny things in your presence, too. Some you heard and never bothered to jot down. Some you've forgotten you ever heard. Some you didn't notice, but you will if you're conscious of gathering comedy.

Your antenna will be up and you'll hear many more of the goofy things that all of us say.

4. Jokes that make the rounds: Sometimes people say goofy things on purpose, too. They usually begin with, "Have you heard the one about?" or "Stop me if you've heard this one." Just try and stop them. "Yes, I did hear that joke." They go on. "It's the one where the guy says, 'Do you know how to light a butane stove?'" You give them the punchline and they still continue. Then they deliver the punchline you just delivered to them—the same punchline you've heard many times before—you laugh politely. Then you probably say to them, "Have you heard *this* one about . . . ." They have heard it, but you tell it anyway.

This is a raconteur's ritual that resembles two rams butting heads fighting for mating rights. It's probably just about as painful, too. Some usable material comes to light occasionally, though. When you hear one that should be included in your list of "potentials," jot down the punchline and enough key words to remind you what the punchline means. That's important.

I recently got a call from Bob Hope. He wanted to know the set-up to a joke I had written ending with the punchline, "with the zipper in front." It's hard to imagine anyone forgetting the straight to that bizarre a punch. I recalled the joke, but I couldn't remember what went before it, either. So as powerful as a joke is at the moment, make sure you also note the preamble to it. Be sure that months from now, the punchline will still make sense.

The joke we researched, incidentally, was about football. It went:

"When I was a kid, my nickname used to be 'Crazy Legs' Hope until I was 15 years old. Then at age 16, I finally learned to put my pants on with the zipper in front."

In using "public domain" material, it's wise to try it out on a few acquaintances first. You don't want to be telling too many stories that are worn, old, tired. There's nothing wrong with telling used jokes, even if a few of the folks in the audience have heard them. But try to avoid including too many that almost everyone in the audience has heard.

5. Joke books: This is probably the most used reference source for humor. You need a joke on doctors, so you turn to the "D" section. There is Dancing, Daughters, Death, Dentists, Divorce, ah . . . there it is, Doctors on page 273. You turn to that page and begin reading through five or six pages of doctor jokes. "I went to the doctor the other day and told him my problem. He said, 'Have you ever had that before?' I said, 'Yeah.' He said, 'Well, you got it again.'" "I told the doctor I had something in my eye. He said, 'Did your mother ever have something in her eye?' I said, 'Yeah.' He said, 'Did your father ever have something in his eye?' I said, 'Yeah.' He said, 'There's your problem. It's hereditary.'"

None of the other 198 jokes apply to your needs any better than those two, so you turn to another book and repeat the process.

You don't like any of the selections in that book, either, so you begin looking under different categories. How about Medicine, Hospitals, maybe Nurses will yield something that can be changed to Doctors?

There's nothing wrong with joke books as a humor source. The research procedure I've described, though, is time consuming. Also, you get so weary of jokes after a while that you begin to lose your judgment. Nothing seems funny, so you might be passing up usable material through mental fatigue. Your funny bone wears out.

The best way to use a joke book is in short spurts. Select different topics to read through in your spare time. If any joke strikes you or seems to be one that you might find useful in a speech, put a check mark next to it. Later, in another free moment, read through and check off jokes from another section. You're more relaxed as you read this way, and you're building up a repertoire. When you desperately need some humor, you don't have to read through the entire volume. You just glance over those you've already checked.

If you're really energetic, you might retype some of your selections into your personal collection. More on that later.

6. Joke services: Joke services are newsletters that publish, usually monthly, a collection of one-liners, stories, anecdotes, and jokes, for use by disc jockeys, speakers, anyone who wants some up-to-date humor. They have an advantage over joke books since they're more current and quicker to read. The same principle applies, though. Read through them and select only those jokes that you like or feel might be usable in the future. Copy those into your own collection and discard the rest.

Most people complain to me that the percentage of usable material they get from these publications hardly justifies the subscription fee. That's relative. If you need a steady supply of fresh material, these might be worthwhile for you. If you don't, the books, though the material is generally weaker and more dated, might be the only source you need.

However, don't judge comedy material by the percentage. The quality of what you get is important—not how much you have to wade through to get it. If you need material and you get enough good lines from a service, don't worry about how many lines you can't use.

7. Books of quotes and sayings: We've discussed the fear of humor in this book already, and I've conceded that the fear is not unfounded. I've written for many comedians who were willing to pay good money for sharp, current, original humor. Then when they went onstage they relied on their tested material. They were afraid to do the original stuff.

Speakers are like that, too. They don't want to take a chance on new material, regardless of how smart it is. "Give me a joke that's already gotten laughs," they say, perhaps without realizing they're saying it.

Well, if you want proven material, written by the best, and tested on countless audiences, try a book of quotes.

In my speaking, I tell my audiences not to take themselves too seriously. Listen to Bertrand Russell saying pretty much the same thing: "One of the symptoms of an approaching nervous breakdown is the belief that one's work is terribly important."

If you're exhorting your charges to be optimistic, these anonymous words might help: "An optimist is someone who starts a crossword puzzle with a fountain pen."

If instead you're cautioning people against being too optimistic, what Don Marquis wrote may be worth repeating: "An optimist is a guy that has never had much experience."

Maybe you're responding to criticism. George Burns had some words that might apply: "Too bad all the people who know how to run the country are busy driving taxicabs and cutting hair."

Somebody at some time has said something witty about whatever you're talking about. You can pass that along to your audience and hear a few laughs as you do.

8. Magazines: *Reader's Digest* has several departments devoted exclusively to humor along with the many fillers that are sprinkled throughout their pages. Those humorous departments always finish first, second, and third in their monthly reader surveys. *McCalls*, until recently, used to end each issue with a page devoted to humor. *Playboy* has a full page of jokes, along with cartoons, in each issue. Many magazines have a section devoted to comedy or small humorous items spaced throughout each issue.

A few of these stories and jokes, or variations on them, could be helpful in adding humor to your communication. It might be wise to read some of these magazines with a pair of scissors at the ready. Snip those items that you like and file them for future use.

9. Regular items in the daily paper: I read a column in the sports section of the *Los Angeles Times* called "Morning Briefing." It's a collection of short items about sports. Often the column will offer colorful quotes. It was in that column that I first read Casey Stengel's directive to his players at spring training: "All right, everybody line up alphabetically according to height." "Morning Briefing" listed Yogi Berra's reply when someone asked his opinion of a New York restaurant. He said, "Nobody goes there anymore. It's too crowded." I read in that column about a 5'6" sports reporter who interviewed Spud Webb, the 5'7" NBA guard who had just won the slam dunk contest. The reporter wanted to know how he, too, could learn to dunk the ball. Webb told him, "Grow an inch."

Many columns like this regularly contain at least one humorous item. Clip it and save it.

10. Listen to comics and other speakers: There's a story about a bunch of New York comedians meeting for lunch. One of the comics mentioned a performer who wasn't present. Someone shouted,

"Don't ever mention that jerk's name in my presence again." "Why, what happened?" the others asked. "That thief is doing my act—the one I stole from Lenny Bruce."

I'm not advocating that you steal some performer's act. But you might be able to get a line, a story, or a joke that will help your communication.

There are some who cry "plagiarism" to me each time I mention this, so perhaps we should discuss the ethics of it now. To me, it's all a matter of degree, and common sense.

Suppose you hear a professional comedian and one of his lines fits in with your message perfectly. Is there any harm in using that line in your speech before 150 of your employees? I doubt that your audiences will ever cross. You're simply not competitors.

If you were a professional comedian and you took lines that another professional paid writers for or wrote himself, then you have an ethics problem. Then you are in competition.

Most professionals have to update their material quickly anyway, because it is passed along by word of mouth. After a while, all the good jokes have been heard. They keep their act flowing, replacing all the lines frequently. Other than their "standard" material—like Gallagher's smashing the watermelon—their lines have a short shelf life.

Professional speakers are different. Many of them have an act that stays the same. They don't wear out material by playing to mass audiences at concerts and on TV. Their good lines aren't heard by as many or passed on as rapidly. Nevertheless, your paths won't cross and you're not in competition with them. An isolated line or story won't harm their careers.

Some speakers confound me. They use material that I know has come from public sources. (Some of it is material I have written.) Then they get peeved if someone uses that line. It's like the guy in the opening story. "Don't ever mention that jerk's name to me again. That thief stole the routine I got out of *Reader's Digest*."

Technically is it plagiarism? I don't know; but I doubt it. I think plagiarism involves more than a single line or story. I do know that within reason there is no harm done, and if a line or two spices up anyone's talk, we professionals in the business of humor should be happy. In my case, I consider it my contribution to the business of humor. I'm delighted when a line I've written is "stolen."

When I worked on the *Jim Nabors Hour*, Phyllis Diller guested and did a monologue that I had written for her right after the first plane hijacking. One of the lines read: "There are three ways to travel now—first class, tourist, and prisoner."

Two writers on the show also wrote for Jack Benny. I read a review of Jack's opening in Las Vegas, and that line was quoted. I confronted the writers. I said, "Benny opened with one of the jokes Phyllis did on this show." One of them said, "Which line?" I told him and he said, "Oh, that line has been around for years." Pretty progressive joke writing, since hijackings had only been around for a few months.

That was a problem because Jack didn't know where the line came from and it could be embarrassing for two well-known professionals to be doing the same material.

If there is no conflict, though, use a good joke in your speaking. Attribute it, if you can. As A.P. Herbert said (see page 81) of this book:

> "There is no good reason why a joke should not be appreciated more than once."

How you collect, file, and cross-reference the material you gather, depends on how meticulous and organized you are. Today's computers and lightning fast data base systems might make it easier for you. However, an index card system still works efficiently, too. I know some people who just paste clippings and jot punchlines into an ever-expanding notebook.

That's up to you. The important thing is that you become aware of the humor around you. Tune into it and gather it. Make sure you jot down enough of it to recall it when you want it. Nothing is more frustrating than a dangling punchline.

CHAPTER TWELVE

How Do I Make the Humor Pertinent?

Neil "Doc" Simon is a former gag writer who parlayed his skills into a lucrative career as a playwright—probably the most successful comedy writer in Broadway history. Several TV writers were discussing their profession one day when one of them suggested that writing was largely inspiration. "Ideas," he claimed, "just float around waiting to be plucked from the air." Another writer agreed but added, "How come they all float over Doc Simon's house?"

There was a story (probably apocryphal) about Doc visiting his old neighborhood in New York. He was at the peak of his success with several hits running concurrently on Broadway, a few movies of his past plays in the theatres, television offers, and an income in the $25,000 a week guestimate range. He stopped in the candy store where he hung out as a youngster. The same owner was there and recognized the alumnus. "Doc," he said, "Doc Simon—how are you?" Simon greeted him and they exchanged pleasantries. The store owner asked, "So what are you doing nowadays, Doc?" Simon said, "I write plays for Broadway." "Yeah," the man was interested. "How much you make doing that?" Doc Simon answered, "About $25,000 a week." The store owner said, "You know, I should have gone into that kind of work."

Obviously, you don't simply "go into that kind of work" and pull down 25 grand a week. Your income depends on how well you use your talent and what you do with the end product. Neil Simon is an excellent example. He was a successful television comedy writer, making an above average salary. Yet, in his spare time he wrote a play on speculation. It was largely autobiographical, titled *Come Blow Your*

Horn. That was his first hit and it was followed, and is still being followed, by many others.

The same applies to material. A funny chunk is just a funny chunk until you apply it. In the last chapter you learned how to gather material. In this chapter we'll discuss how to apply the material you've stockpiled to your particular message.

Humor can be very flexible. It can contain many messages. I remember once having to read Ernest Hemingway's *The Old Man and the Sea.* It's a short but powerful book and well worth reading. This was a schoolwork assignment, though, and I had to write an evaluation of the story. I went to the library and picked up several books explaining Hemingway's book. It seemed odd to me that this tiny volume would have so many books discussing the author's meaning. Each of these books was three times as large as the original work.

I had the same feeling watching a basketball game on television. It was a close game and one of the coaches called a time out. The two announcers then explained the coach's strategy for the call. "He's trying to stop the other team's momentum," one said. His partner added, "That plus his team is exhausted from that incredible comeback. He wanted to give them a rest." The first went on, "He also realizes that there is a mandatory time out coming shortly, so this is his brilliant way of getting an extra rest period in." The next said, "Also, this is a critical part of the game right now and he probably wants to make sure they understand the strategy." They both went on until they had offered about twelve separate reasons for the time out. One or two of them might have been valid, but only a genius coach could have thought through twelve or more reasons.

The point I'm making is that jokes, stories, anecdotes—any piece of humor—can contain many lessons. They can be applied many different ways. Even though you exhaust all possible applications—if there is a limit—you can change the story slightly and generate even more.

Let's look at an example of this. I've heard the next story attributed to many people, so I'll attribute it to none. I'll just generalize. The story goes:

> A referee penalized a team for unnecessary roughness. As he
> marched off the 15 yards, one of the angry players berated

him. He came right to the referee's nose and shouted, "You stink."

The ref calmly picked up the ball and paraded downfield another 15 yards. He turned to the player and yelled, "How do I smell from here?"

That's the anecdote. Now let's play like our chatty sports announcers and devise some messages that the story might contain. To keep track, we'll number them.

1) It might be used as an illustration for an executive standing by his decisions. This official made a call. He believed it was the right call. When a massive football player challenged him, did he fold? No, he stood by his call. He stood by it so strongly that he made another call. He tacked on another 15 yards for unsportsmanlike conduct.

2) This story might show how a leader must be in charge. He must remain strong. He might have made a marginal call. He might have made a bad call. What's important is that he made a call. He called it as he saw it and he kept control of the game by standing by that call.

3) There's a lesson in that story for the "players," too. Don't compound mistakes. The first penalty was an error that the team paid dearly for. Fifteen yards is a steep price in a hard-fought football game. But when one player lost his cool, he turned a 15-yarder into a 30-yarder. Learn to accept the mistakes you make in the heat of battle, put them behind you, and continue playing hard.

4) You pay for your errors. Football teams pay on the field with a loss of yardage when they commit a foul. The referee withdraws yardage that they worked hard to earn. They might have gotten away with this infraction once or twice, but eventually the whistle blew. They were penalized. To make matters worse they were penalized again. The same happens in life and in the office. You can't get away for too long with shortcuts. You either do the job right or eventually you suffer the consequences.

5) Sometimes you have to accept the injustices of life quietly and learn to work with them. The first penalty in this story might have been a bad call. However, the damage was done; the 15 yards were measured against them. The smart thing to do now would be to earn back those subtracted yards. To rail against the official—to fight City

Hall—only caused more distress. The satisfaction of telling him "You stink" was hardly worth another 15 yards.

There are five different applications of the same anecdote. With minimal thought you could probably convert that to an even half-dozen. With a little more thinking you might make a dozen. The possibilities, as the cliche goes, are endless.

It's not important that you like this particular anecdote or agree that it's funny. Do you see how it is flexible? That's the message. Those stories that you collect—the ones you do like—can be just as utilitarian.

There are two ways of finding humor that is apropos to your message:

1) Find a story you like that fits.

2) Find a story you like and make it fit.

It's important to notice in both of these methods that you first have to know what you want to say. You have to have your point clear in your head before you can illustrate or reinforce it. I heard a joke on radio as a kid that I still remember (and occasionally borrow) today. In a crisis within the show's story, Red Skelton offered this maxim: "Just remember, the young tree bends, while the old tree can bend or break." Someone asked, "What does that mean?" Skelton said, "I don't know, but it cheers me up."

Unfortunately, as speakers, we have to know what we're trying to say, and then say it. Why were Abraham Lincoln's stories so pertinent? Probably because he knew exactly what he wanted to say. That's always Step One.

Experiment #1

Now let's see how the two methods work with a particular message. Let's suppose that you are speaking to a group of people who have been opposed to your principles. In two previous encounters these people have sided with your antagonist. You want to chide them gently, but not alienate them. Ideally, you want to convert them.

That's our mock premise for this experiment. If you want to try it, take a break now and read through some of the material you've collected. Find out if you have anything that fits. If not, run through your mind, and see if you can uncover some story or anecdote that is apropos here. Failing that, look in your quote book and see if someone has said something about it in the past. I don't know what heading you'd look under, but try several. It's good practice.

Have you come up with anything yet? I found a quote I had stashed away that applies with a little manipulation. It was from a man recently appointed as the new basketball coach at the local college. Another coach had turned down the offer, so the reporters asked, "Does it bother you that you were the school's second choice?" He said, "Not at all, I was my wife's second choice and we've been together 34 years."

That could be changed to: "Don't feel bad about changing your mind, because I don't. I know you've turned me down twice before; but you know, my wife turned me down twice before she agreed to marry me and we've been together for 34 years."

But here's how John Kennedy uncovered a story that fit perfectly. JFK was campaigning in Texas, a state that had voted Republican (for Eisenhower) in the last two elections. Kennedy said to the crowd:

> "There's a story about a Texan who went to New York and told a New Yorker that he could jump off the Empire State Building and live. The easterner said, "Well, that would be an accident." He said, "Suppose I did it twice?" The easterner said, "That would be an accident, too." "Suppose I did it three times?" And the easterner said, "That would be a habit."

Kennedy continued, "Texas twice jumped off the Democratic band wagon. We are down here to see it is not going to be a habit."

We've seen how a quote and an anecdote seemed to fit the message we had. Let's pick a different topic for our second experiment—making a story fit our message.

Experiment #2

Let's suppose that our talk in this experiment is about belt-tightening. You're trying to convince workers to be more conscious of costs. Now take some time to review your favorite stories or bits of humor and see if you can mold some of them to fit naturally into this premise.

Give it some effort because it is a worthwhile exercise. How'd you do? Here's one I came up with:

You can find ways to save considerable amounts of money without going overboard. I guess the greatest moneysaver I ever heard about was the man who was on an aircraft that experienced lots of turbulence. This man wasn't crazy about flying in the first place, but when this plane began bumping around the skies, he really got scared. He started to pray. He said, 'Lord, I'm a rich man. But if you let this plane land safely, Lord, I'll give you half of everything I own. Just get me on the ground, Lord, and I'll split everything with you, fifty-fifty.' Well, the plane did land safely and this man was the first one off. As he walked along in the airport, a preacher tapped him on the shoulder. He said, 'Sir, I was on that plane with you and I heard what you said. You said if the Lord let the plane land safely you would give him half of all you own. Well, I'm a man of the cloth and I'm here to collect.' The man said, 'No, I made the Lord a better deal. I told him if He ever catches me on a plane again, He can have it all.'

That's the trick to it—as easy as 1-2-3. (1) Know what you want to say. (2) Find something in your collection that says it perfectly. (3) If nothing says it quite that well, find the hidden message in some of your other material, or bend it slightly so that it does suit your purpose.

There's a fourth option, but it deserves a chapter of its own. That option is to write your own material.

CHAPTER THIRTEEN

Can I Really Write My Own?

Many years ago, several colleagues roasted Jack Benny. The affair was a surprise to Jack. At the banquet, many speakers kidded their friend with the putdown humor typical of a roast. The guest of honor, of course, was allowed the last word—the rebuttal, so to speak. When Jack reached the microphone he said, "You wouldn't have said all those nasty things about me if my writers were here."

Appearing at a television writers' awards banquet, Bob Hope commented, "Most people outside the business think that I make up all these jokes. And let's keep it that way."

Both comedians were graciously paying tribute to their creative staffs; both were also saluting original material. Often the best and quickest solution to your humor needs is to write your own.

I can almost hear your arguments coming through the pages of this book now. "Benny and Hope weren't writing their own material. They were buying material." That's true, but it's a technicality. Both performers have participated in the writing and editing of their material. They needed such great quantities of humor that they had to hire staffs to provide it. Nevertheless, the material was designed for them, and often for specific occasions. Essentially, it was their material.

That leads to another dispute, though. "How can you expect me to write my own material, when such great talents as Hope and Benny have to hire top professionals to write theirs? Surely they're naturally funnier than I am." Probably, but there are several reasons why that shouldn't dissuade you from writing your own.

First, professional performers like Hope and Benny need much more material than you do, and they need it quickly. None of the top pros can turn out the quantity and the quality of the material they require without help. You can. Where Bob Hope might require 50 to 75 new, pertinent one-liners for a banquet this evening and the same amount for a concert tomorrow evening, you might only require three incisive lines for a speech you're giving next week. You've got time to work on that.

Second, you don't have to be as funny as Hope or any other comic performer. Show business says, "You're only as good as your last performance." These professionals are measured by how funny they are. You're not. You're measured by how well you convey your message. Humor is a tool to help you convey that message effectively.

Third, you have the potential to be funnier than Hope or his writers. How? By knowing more about your audience than they would. The sharper the focus is on your material, the more it hits the audience, the funnier it is. Hope especially works hard to keep his material localized. As I'm writing this chapter, I received a call from Mr. Hope for special material for a concert he's doing for "Weed-eater" salesmen. That's the gardening device that trims in hard-to-reach places and such. So he'll do material like the following:

> "That weed-eater is a great invention. I carry one in my golf-bag."
>
> "When I get that thing working right, I can *putt* out of the rough.
>
> "The weed-eater has helped my golf game in the past, but now I'm ready to move up to odor-eaters."

That material is localized, but it's not nearly as on-the-mark as you can be. You might know that some guy in the third row of your audience had car trouble on the way home from work last night. You might be aware of the big winner in last week's poker game. If you have this kind of inside information, it can help you generate usable humor that is funnier and more insightful than the pros'.

The Benefits of Writing Your Own Humor

1. It's fresher: Self-generated humor is usually obvious, and I don't mean that as a put-down. Just the opposite. You know the way you can tell just by looking whether a pie is home-baked or store-bought. That's how an audience can sense original humor. They sense it and they appreciate it. Often it doesn't even have to be as good as the store-bought variety. With both baking and comedy writing, people respect the work that went into it.

I once emceed a company party. The affair was held at a nearby restaurant immediately after work. When I approached the microphone, it whistled. (Some of the controls were set too high which generated feedback, or some such technical explanation like that. I don't know. I just talk into microphones; I don't explain them.) I backed off and the humming stopped. I stepped forward and got more shrill noise. This happened a few times until the manager noticed the problem and adjusted the controls. Finally, I could approach the mike without that deafening sound. My first words were: "I'm sorry about that, but when you hold the banquet right after work, I don't always get a chance to shower first."

That opener got a big laugh and applause. Why? Was it that hilarious a joke? No. It was, though, an obvious ad-lib. There was no way it could have been pre-arranged, and the audience knew and acknowledged that.

2. It's your style: The best humor, and we'll discuss this in the following chapter, always has your trademark on it. It reflects your point of view, your sense of humor, and your speaking style. If you write it, those things will most likely be a part of it.

Let me use another example from my office emceeing days. This was a negative, but you might as well learn from my mistakes.

I was hosting a banquet for an accountant who was retiring, so I "borrowed" a Bob Newhart routine about the office retirement party. I didn't steal the routine because in the preamble, I mentioned that it was from Newhart's album, but thought the audience would appreciate it in this context. It's a very funny monologue and was particularly apropos at this affair, but it didn't do well at all. The audience laughed at all the right places because it was a very tight, funny routine; but afterwards, several people told me, "Do your own stuff from now on. It's funnier."

I must clarify that remark for Mr. Newhart's sake. I don't want to antagonize him by claiming to be funnier than him. They meant that

I was funnier doing my material—the stuff they were used to—than I was doing Bob Newhart's routines. The jokes I wrote and performed were my style; the Newhart routines were Newhart's style.

The closer we can get our material to our own personality and speaking style, the better it will be. You can accomplish that to a degree by writing your own.

3. It's to the point: We've seen previously that some of your humor must be pertinent—not all of it, but some of it. It can be an agonizing search to find that perfect piece of material to fit the point you're trying to make. It's like trying to shop for the perfect home. You always end up compromising somewhere. One room is too small or the yard isn't designed as you pictured it. Something is off a touch. If we could all design our own dream houses they would be just that—dream houses.

You can design your own "dream humor." Write it yourself. Create a story or joke that says exactly what you want it to say.

4. It's funnier because it's focused: Some wit once described a specialist as "a doctor who knows more and more about less and less." That applies also to a good punchline. You want to narrow your attack down as much as you can. You want to say something very meaningful (and funny) about as isolated a group as you can.

Mark Russell may say something very witty about our politicians. That's great. Political humor applies to all Americans. A speaker, though, addressing a convention may make a remark about how politics affect this specific association. All things being equal, the specific gag will be more effective. A speaker from the group may do a joke about the politics of the gentleman sitting to his right. Now you have a joke focused right on the president of the association, good old Harry. If it's a funny line, it's a powerful joke because everybody loves to kid good old Harry.

Another example from my office toastmastering days. (I use these because all were times that I was writing my own material and it was highly localized.) I spoke from the head table. The guest of honor and his wife sat immediately to my right. Everyone could see their reactions to the humor. Also, everyone knew that this gentleman had three children who were accomplished musicians, all played in highly respected concert orchestras. The children were at a table up front. I said, "George and his wife have three children who are great musicians. George wanted a piano player, so he and his wife had a little boy. Then they wanted a violin player, so they had a little girl. Then they wanted a trumpet player, so they had another boy. You should have seen the look on his wife's face when George came home from work one day singing '76 Trombones.'"

The audience was looking at the people I was talking about and not only reacting to the joke, but reacting to the principals reacting to the joke. The closer you can come to that kind of focus, the more effective your humor will be.

A word of caution, though. Don't narrow the attack down so much that the audience is not in on the joke. In speaking to national associations, I often ask for some inside information. "Give me the scuttlebutt," I tell the program chairman. They do, but sometimes it's only scuttlebutt that the people on the executive board are aware of. The other 750 people that comprise the audience don't know what the hell I'm talking about.

Don't make your material so specialized that only a select few will appreciate it. You have to reach the entire audience.

5. It's original: You'll never hear anyone from your audience say, "We had a speaker in last week who told that same delightful story."

All right, I told you a few chapters back where and how to look for material. And now I'm telling you that your own writing is superior. Why did I ask you to look up the other stuff?

You need to build up a repertoire of usable material, because like the pros, you're not always going to have the time to create all the material you need as quickly as you need it. So it's important to have a dependable backlog of material to fall back on.

Your files, too, can be a springboard for ideas for your own writing. Glancing through the material you've already researched can stimulate your thinking along similar lines. You may be inspired to write new material on the same topics or incorporate the same ideas as your stock material.

For example, when we're assigned to write material for Bob Hope and the jokes just aren't coming, some of us read through past material or watch video tapes of previous monologues. Getting involved in the form and style inspires us to create new Bob Hope one-liners.

Most importantly, though, you can use your writing skills in conjunction with the material you research. When you gather jokes, stories, anecdotes, and such, you're compiling raw material. You're stockpiling the lumber. Eventually, you have to get out the hammer and nails to build the new dog house.

You want to take each of the items you collected and tailor them to suit your style and needs. Let's look at an example. Here is a standard joke that you may or may not have heard. It has been around, but here's the way I might tailor it if I were to use it in my presentation:

> There's a little bar across the street from CBS where I've spent most of my writing career—at CBS, not at the bar.
>
> I usually stop in there for a cocktail or two after work, because with the freeway system in Los Angeles, if I leave work at 5 or 5:30, it might take me 50 or 60 minutes to get home. But if I go to this bar and sit there until . . . like . . . 11:30—no traffic at all.
>
> This place is really a CBS hangout. Cameramen, writers, producers, stars, all go over there. We know one another, and we kid one another. Rarely does a "civilian" come into the place.
>
> One time, I was sitting in the bar and a friend introduced me to a guest from out of town—his cousin from Green Bay, Wisconsin. So, I kidded. I said, "I only heard of two things from Green Bay, Wisconsin—great football players and terrible hookers."
>
> Just then a guy tapped me on the shoulder—a civilian— a big civilian. He said, "Hey pal, my wife's from Green Bay, Wisconsin."
>
> I said, "Really? What position does she play?"

There's a standard joke that became "my" story with some writing. The joke is no longer "two guys went into a bar." It's now about "my" bar. I added a few simple jokes up front (" . . . CBS—not the bar" and " . . . until . . . like . . . 11:30").

The story and the punchline are still the same, but the set-up has been altered with creative writing.

You can utilize your creative writing talents, too, in "switching" stories. "Switching," which is done often in comedy writing and is perfectly acceptable, means to take a joke or story you've heard or seen somewhere else and change it around enough so that it becomes a new joke. In effect, you use either the punchline or the premise of the original to generate a new gag.

To give you an example here is a joke from many years ago, followed by a few of the "switches."

Original

PANHANDLER: Can you give me a buck for a cup of coffee?
MAN: What do you need a buck for? Coffee is only a dime.
PANHANDLER: Can I help it if I'm a big tipper?

Some Switches

PANHANDLER: Can you give me a dime for a cup of coffee and make it quick?
MAN: What's your hurry?
PANHANDLER: I'm double-parked.

PANHANDLER: Can you give me $2000 for a cup of coffee?
MAN: $2000! Coffee is only a dime.
PANHANDLER: I want to drink it in Tahiti.

PANHANDLER: Can you give me 10 cents for a cup of coffee and $10 to catch a show?
MAN: What do you mean $10 to catch a show?
PANHANDLER: Coffee keeps me awake late. I have to have something to do.

Here's another example of a joke and switches:

Original

It's easy to spot Jerry Ford's golf cart. It's the one with the big red cross on top.

Switches

It's easy to spot Jerry Ford's golf cart. It's the one with the coin-operated insurance machine on the back.

It's easy to spot Jerry Ford's golf cart. It's the only one with an air-raid shelter attached behind it.

The above examples are all switches on the punchline, using the same basic premise or set-up. The switch can also take place in the set-up, though, with the punchline remaining practically the same.

Here are some examples:

Original

You know I always hear comedians say, "A funny thing happened to me on the way to the theatre tonight," then they tell a joke. I've been doing comedy for 30 years and nothing funny ever happened to me on the way to the theatre . . . until tonight.

Switches

I've heard many people say that they're afraid to face an audience. I've been speaking for a long time and I've never once met an audience that frightened me . . . until tonight.

(This one is purely in fun, to kid someone on the dais, but it works if you follow it up properly)

I've sat at the head table for many banquets and I've met a lot of people—men, women; big shots, small shots; blue and white collar workers—and I can honestly say I've never met a person I didn't like . . . until tonight.

Don't be afraid to tinker with the material that you've assembled. The jokes and stories in your files are there to serve your needs. They're like the family dog: they become better pets when they do what they're told. With some inventive writing, you can make your collection of humor do exactly what you want it to do.

Writing humor is not nearly as mysterious and difficult as most comedy writers pretend it is. The intangibles of talent and creativity are involved, but there is also a step-by-step procedure that you can follow. There is no guarantee, of course, that following the steps will produce lines like Woody Allen's or Mort Sahl's, but they will guide you in getting the most out of your comedy writing skills.

Remember, too, that you don't have to be as good as Allen or Sahl. Your lines will have added impact because no one expects you to be a humorist. Jim Nabors became a vocalist because as Gomer Pyle no one expected him to sing. When he did sing, and sing well, many people exaggerated their reaction. "He really sings great!" That means, "He really sings great compared to how I expected him to sing." Understand, I'm not belittling Jim's vocalizing. I'm simply saying that because of the Gomer Pyle character he played, the initial reaction to his singing was magnified. That worked to Jim's benefit and it can work to yours.

You don't need as much material as Woody Allen or Mort Sahl, either. The small amount of humor that you do should be received more appreciatively because you are closer to your audience and should be able to do material that will "hit them right between the eyes."

The Writing Process

1.

The first step in the writing process is often overlooked even though it is the most obvious. You have to have something to talk about.

If someone came to me and said, "Write me a joke," my first question would be, "About what?" If the client can't answer that, or doesn't care to, I have to answer it for the client. I have to supply my own topic. I can't create a joke unless I first know what I want to joke about.

It's like someone asking you, "What did you think of the movie?" You say, "Which movie?" They say, "Oh, I don't care. Any one." You can't give an opinion until you decide which film you'll critique.

The very first decision you must make is what you're going to comment on. You have to select a topic, a premise, or at least an area that you will think about.

2.

The next step is analytical and investigative. You have to gather information about your topic. Sometimes this requires research—talking to people or looking data up in a book—but often it's a matter of organizing the information you already have.

I recommend getting that information in visible form in front of you. Take a few minutes to jot down key words and phrases, maybe a few statements, about your topic. Just doodle on a scratch pad. This gets the information out of your head and onto paper. It frees your mind for the creative process as opposed to the remembering process.

Be prolific. Write anything and everything that comes to your mind. Don't worry about being selective, yet. You won't use all of the information that you gather, but you will find some of it helpful. How? Well, let's study a few short, simple jokes:

> "Income tax has made more liars out of the American people than golf has."
>
> Will Rogers

> "To give you an idea how fast we travelled; we left Spokane with two rabbits and when we got to Topeka, we still had only two."
>
> Bob Hope

> "Beverly Hills is very exclusive. For instance, their fire department doesn't make house calls."
>
> Mort Sahl

> "It's a recession when your neighbor loses his job, it's a depression when you lose your own."
>
> Harry S Truman

> "When I was young it was wine, women and song; now it's Metrecal, my old gal, and 'Sing along with Mitch.'"
>
> Any number of comedians

These are five varied comments on divergent topics by different people. Yet they all have one thing in common. They are comparisons of two different ideas. Will Rogers compares the tax to golf. Hope uses rabbits and their mating habits to measure the speed of travel. Mort Sahl likens a fire department to a doctor to show exclusivity. Truman contrasts a recession to a depression. The last gag compares youth to old age. There are exceptions, but basically these comparisons are the heart of spoken humor.

Johnny Carson's gimmick illustrates that. He says, "Boy, it was hot in Burbank today." The audience shouts, "How hot was it?" "It was so hot that . . . " and he compares the Burbank weather to something, anything bizarre.

Most jokes compare two ideas that are either (wait till you hear this for an all-inclusive statement) very different, slightly different, or exactly the same. In Rogers' comment golf is similar to taxes. Hope says that his travel time was exactly the same as the length of time that two rabbits can control themselves. Sahl says the Beverly Hills fire department is the same as their doctors. Truman says a recession is slightly different from a depression (or in an ironic way, it's very much different—depends on your point of view). The last gag certainly says that age is different from youth.

Your sheet of information serves two purposes in the creative process. First it's a springboard to these comparisons. What you jot down can prompt you to create comparisons. The process of thinking as you write is beneficial, also: The data on the page may jump out at you. Two items may be quite similar or different. There's your irony.

For example, let's just fantasize that you were trying to write a line about present day economics—as Truman did. In your jottings, you might list "friends lose their jobs." Later on the page you write, "I lose my job." Bingo! There's the difference between a recession and a depression.

Second, some item on your page may be the solution to an unresolved comparison. You have the first piece of your puzzle—something that you want to say. Now what do you compare it to? The answer may be on that page of notes you've scribbled.

You know that Carson's writers make a list of things that will graphically and humorously answer the audience question, "How hot was it?" Hope's writer searched for something that goes by "fast." It turned out to be rabbit abstinence.

Let me illustrate how I use this research to help generate jokes. You can work along with me. Make your own list and generate some of your own lines. You'll see how the research makes the writing easier. Also you may notice that two people using the same basic procedure on the same topic can create lines that are very much different.

Let's say I want to come up with some funny lines that I might use in a promotional piece for this book. I want to kid—do some roast type of material—about my own writing. You're invited to join in, too.

First I start with free association. I list any ideas that have a possible connection to books and authors. I don't edit myself or second guess my selections; I just jot them down. I certainly won't use all of them to write jokes, but they're there for those jokes that I do write.

Why don't you make a list, too, before reading mine?

My list might be:

Dust jacket, "cover to cover," "couldn't put it down,"
autographed copy, autograph party, typographical errors,
proofread, best-seller, picture on the back cover, reviews,
large print, good writing, easy reading, bookshelf, gift item,
complimentary copy, royalties, subtitles, cover price, book
stores, bookstore clerk, and so on.

After the exercise, I focus my thinking even more. I attack the
thought process in a more orderly way. I make a list of people, places,
things, events, and cliches that are similar to my topic. Then I make
a list of the same items that are opposite my topic. Here are some
examples:

Similar

People—Erma Bombeck
　　　　Bob Hope
　　　　Steve Allen

Places— bookstore
　　　　bookshelf
　　　　booksellers convention

Things—bookmarks
　　　　bookends
　　　　inscriptions

Events—book sale
　　　　television appearance

Cliches—a real page-turner
　　　　a great book to give someone
　　　　packs a wallop
　　　　I loved the book

Opposite

People—illiterates
　　　　Matthew, Mark, Luke, and John

Places— porno book store
　　　　Christian Science reading room

Things—movies
        videos
        doorstop
        Guinness Book of World Records

Events—tar and feathering
        book burnings

Cliches—I don't read books
        I don't read fiction
        Who wrote it for you?
        I read it in one sitting

Now I use these as ammunition for joke ideas. The "couldn't put it down" association might prompt lines like:

I couldn't put the book down . . . often enough.

I couldn't put the book down. It was clever of Gene to print the dust jacket on flypaper. (That combined another idea from the list—dust jacket.)

(*or a total switch*) It's the kind of a book, once you put it down, you just can't pick it up again.

The idea of an autographed copy intrigued me:

I'm glad the copy Gene gave me was autographed. It was the only good writing in there.

Here's one based on "I loved the book":

My brother said, "I loved the book. Up until now, I was the black sheep of the family."

An idea that originated with the "gift idea":

Gene's book makes a great gift item. It sure beats keeping it yourself.

Here's one generated by the "Who wrote it for you" insult:

A friend read my book and asked me "Who wrote it for you?" I asked him, "Who read it to you?"

I think you can readily see how this mental research, this thinking and jotting down of related topics and items supplies valuable raw materials—and even generates ideas—for humor.

The next step is to get the joke ideas flowing. Unless you've gotten lucky in the first few procedures, you haven't really written any material yet; you've just organized your thinking. That's commendable and a necessary prerequisite. Eventually, though, you have to get something on paper. How do you start writing funny?

Two procedures that will help get your mind creating:

1) Make statements
2) Ask questions

3.

Making statements gives you a very important part of your joke—the first part of your comparison. You make several statements about the topic you're discussing, then you search for a proper "caption" for each statement. You need something to compare it to, something that will make it funny.

This procedure reminds me of captioning pictures. You've seen books like this, and even seen it on the Johnny Carson show, where Carson holds up wacky photos and then captions them. It often gives a whole new meaning to the action in the photo. You do the same thing with a "verbal photo." You try to caption the statement you make.

Let's run through an exercise that will help illustrate this process. Assume that you have to comment on Jim and Tammy Baker. You've researched and gathered information on them and jotted much of it down. Now you make the following statement:

It's reported that Jim and Tammy may open up another church.

That's a true statement as of this writing. They may not open a new ministry. They may not even be thinking of it, but some people have said it so you're safe in saying, "It is reported." Now you have to find something from your research to attach to the tail end of that statement to make it a joke.

Okay, here are some of the possible captions you might put on that fairly innocuous statement to turn it into a joke:

> . . . Tammy wants to call it "Our Lady of Avon."

> . . . Jim wants to get back to preaching; it's a great way to meet girls.

> . . . Jim says it's the only thing he knows how to do well. Jessica Hahn agrees with him.

From this point, you can make another statement on the same topic. For instance, "The church is supposed to be built in Palm Springs." Now find some captions that will work with that statement.

4.

Asking questions often opens up other avenues of creativity that you haven't yet dreamed of. With this device, you open up your topic; you let it ramble into unexplored areas. You play the "who else" or "what if" games with your premise.

Suppose, for example, you're discussing the presidential races, you might get some interesting humorous ideas if you asked "How else could they decide this beside an election?" That might lead to mud wrestling, a golf play-off, a boxing match, a tag team wrestling match, a game of *Jeopardy;* how about a Sumo wrestling match? (No, then Tip O'Neill would surely win.)

You might even wonder, since Ronald Reagan was a former actor, what if other performers ran and were elected President? How would Dean Martin behave in the White House? Sammy Davis? The Smothers Brothers? Well, you see the possibilities.

There are any number of crazy questions you could ask, and each will lead to more and more bizarre answers.

The Hiding Place of Humor

You can follow all of the above steps, do all the practice routines, write and rewrite, and still not come up with any humor. You simply come up with well-researched and organized statements. When do you breathe the fun into it? Where do you look for humor?

Humor is truth and, more often than not, truth is humor. As a beginning jokesmith, I sent many gags to Phyllis Diller. Phyllis's act is as bizarre and far out as one can imagine. Yet, when she sent back one of my submissions marked "Not true!" I couldn't believe it. Phyllis Diller, with the outlandish jokes about her husband and children, couldn't be demanding absolute accountability for each statement in the routine! She was. Then it dawned on me. The premise could be twisted, distorted, bent out of shape, exaggerated, rearranged, or whatever; but it had to be basically true. I could say her mother-in-law was so big that her zip code was also her dress size. That was okay. It was an exaggeration of the truth—her mother-in-law was big. But I couldn't have her reply when her husband complained about replacing the clutch on the family car three times in one year, "Don't blame me. I never use it." Why? Because if she didn't use the clutch, the transmission would be destroyed—not the clutch.

The lesson is, when you're searching for humor, hunt out the truth. Often the truth itself is the humor. I began working as a gagwriter in the 1950's for a black comedian, Slappy White. We did much material about the civil rights movement. Here are two pieces of humor that were basically just true statements:

> "If we've made such great strides in civil rights, let me ask just one thing: How come in that gasoline commercial on television, the black car always runs out of gas before the white one?"

> "I'm not going to participate in those civil rights marches no more. I told the Reverend Martin Luther King, 'You ride the bus. Let me pray awhile.'"

Of course, you can also make the truth flexible. Consider these jokes about Phyllis Diller's mother-in-law, Moby Dick:

> "She's so big, one day she wore a white dress and got mobbed. A group of kids mistook her for a Good Humor truck."

> "She wore a red, white, and blue dress one day. She was standing on the corner and a man threw a letter in her mouth."

"She wore a grey dress once, and an admiral boarded her."

These are obvious exaggerations. In one gag she's as big as a truck, then the size of a mailbox, and finally as large as a battleship. They can't all be true; in fact, none of them are. The basic premise is, though—that she is large.

The trick here is to look for the truth, the real truth, and nothing but the truth. Sometimes protocol, tradition, and etiquette hide the truth. They do such a good job that we often lose track of reality altogether. A veneer covers the facts and is often mistaken for them. Humor results from exposing that hidden reality.

Politicians present a facade of unswerving patriotism and impeccable ethics. They pretend to be above politics. We know better.

How about the TV evangelists who fiercely condemned adultery? We had fun peeling away that veneer.

Not all disguises are that grand. Most are everyday, mundane "little white lies." For example, there's the well-dressed business man in his dark power suit and red tie who is wearing frayed underwear. How about the bad tennis player who has been hitting the ball poorly for 15 years, yet after each bad shot he glares at his racket as if it were the culprit.

We're all guilty of it. We all live little deceptions daily. And exposing the fraud is fun. That's why the pie in the face was funny when it hit the rich dowager. She thought she was above a cream pie in the kisser. We laughed when Chaplin and Laurel and Hardy proved she wasn't.

The Surprise Element in Humor

Surprise is a tremendously important element of humor. That's why we try to stop anyone who's telling a joke that we heard already. Why try to stop them? The words are the same; so is the story—nothing has changed. Because we've heard it before, though, the surprise has gone out of it. The fun has been removed.

When we do a rewrite, or take another stab at a topic for Bob Hope, he frequently tells me to remind the writers to "hide the joke more." That means to make the punchline more of a surprise. Generally, you accomplish that by playing with the wording of your gag. You have a good premise, and two ideas that compare well. But you can't just state them, you have to say them in a funny way, a different way. Like the jazz musician who gave his two weeks' notice to the bandleader this way: "Four weeks from now, I will have been gone two."

Most writers maintain that you should always get the punchline as close to the end of the joke as possible. That way the key word in the joke is saved as the real twist or surprise. These lines are good examples:

> At a roast for a gentleman who was kidded about the way he dressed: "He never let success go to his clothing."
>
> At a roast for an actor: "He is to acting what John McEnroe is to tennis—a real pain in the ass."
>
> Bob Hope, telling how he felt about having a street named after him in Burbank: "I'm now the star of stage, screen, and police accident reports."

Notice the joke word or phrase is right at the end, and disguised well until then.

Another way to surprise an audience is by stating your humorous idea by not really stating it. Say it by not saying it. You replace the actual statement by something that implies it. These are examples:

> A man purchasing tickets on an airline that had some recent bad publicity: "I'll take two chances to Chicago, please."
>
> Bob Hope's reply when I asked him how a show's rehearsal went: "I may have to do my vaudeville act."
>
> Here's a basketball coach's reply when asked how he explained his team's 2 win, 17 loss, and 1 tie record: "Well, we overwhelmed two opponents, underwhelmed 17, and whelmed one."

All of these folks said something by not saying it. If your punchlines seem too obvious or too direct—try to deliver the punchline instead with an alternate meaning.

For example, the 1988 Republican Convention televised from New Orleans drew only mediocre ratings. A comic might say, "How can they expect to get people to vote for them, when they can't even get them to watch their convention?"

That's a valid joke idea. It's an ironic comment. Saying it that straightforward, though, it becomes just a flat joke, a statement.

Jay Leno punched it up on the *Tonight Show* this way: "The Republican Convention got very low ratings. How can they expect to beat Dukakis and Bentsen when they can't even beat *Jake and the Fatman?*"

When Bob Hope wanted to say that Gerald Ford was a dangerous golfer, he said it instead with a compliment: "Jerry Ford is a great athlete. I don't know whether you know it or not, but he has a black belt in golf."

They both said what they wanted to say by saying something else. It's an effective way of hiding the punchline.

Think Funny

Thinking funny is an attitude. It's a way of looking at life and not taking it too seriously—especially ourselves. If humor is truth, the enemy of humor is deception, fraud, trying to be something we're not.

Thinking funny is a sort of controlled irreverence—not being over-awed by anything or anybody. In doing humor, the president of the company is as ripe for a one-liner as the guys and gals on the assembly line.

When you analyze and investigate, accept the face value of nothing—in a whimsical, not a cynical, way. Remember we said that a veneer covers most of civilized society. Recognize and scratch away that veneer and you'll begin seeing the humor all around you.

When Will Rogers was going to meet President Coolidge for the first time at a White House reception, friends said that Coolidge was a humorless man. Rogers promised to get an immediate laugh from him.

The President shook the comedian's hand, Rogers whispered something, and Coolidge laughed. What was the magic? When the President introduced himself, Rogers simply said, "I'm sorry. I didn't catch the name." Irreverent, yes—but funny.

Also, look beyond the obvious. Many jokes are built on misunderstanding obvious word patterns. "Can you tell me how long cows should be milked?" "Sure, the same as short ones." The key words in the question are "how long"; the comic hears instead "long cows." Most of Groucho Marx's humor was based on this gimmick. "Last night I shot a lion in my pajamas. How he got in my pajamas, I'll never know."

These are word plays, but there are other ideas hidden beyond the obvious, too. Finding them can uncover humor. Dig into topics and premises and find out the why and the wherefore. Sometimes that's the real fun of the topic.

Consider the way comedian Jackie Mason had fun by looking beyond the explanation for sex scenes in motion pictures. He said, "Every movie you see today has a sex scene. It doesn't have anything to do with anything; it's just in there. They explain that by saying, 'People do that.' Well, people eat soup, too, but you don't see a bowl of soup in every movie."

Will Rogers said, "We are all here for a spell, get all the good laughs you can." That's the attitude that helps you see reality, truth, humor. And, whenever you see something funny—even if you have to look for it real hard—write it down!

CHAPTER FOURTEEN

Put Yourself Into Your Humor

When Red China opened the door to visitors, Bob Hope was one of the first entertainers to tape a show there. The American papers reported extensively about the problems Hope had with his translator. Some phrases didn't translate well, some the interpreter couldn't translate because he didn't know what they meant, some he misunderstood and misinterpreted. It made most of the front pages.

Hope called me from China, and I questioned him about it. He said, "I did a show in the afternoon and no one was laughing. Nobody in the audience spoke English. So I called my interpreter out. I'd do a joke and get nothing. Then he'd translate it, and get giant laughs. At the evening show, a lot of the American workers were there—most of the people spoke English. At that show, I got screams. This other guy was getting nothing."

I love that story for many reasons. First, I picture this interpreter who had never heard of Bob Hope, nor seen any of his work. He has to come onstage,—not the easiest thing for a non-performer to do—tell jokes that he doesn't fully understand, and get laughs that were never meant for him. If you ever want to define the word "confusion," this gentleman's attitude would probably do it for you.

Second, I enjoy the legendary Bob Hope feeling slightly envious because another "performer" is getting his laughs, then being satisfied at the evening show when he "got even."

The interpreter, though, was doing his job, and presumably doing it well. He was repeating the words exactly as he heard them. That was his job; it's not yours.

There's a story about an inept actor performing—very badly—the lead in a Shakespearean play. The audience was offended by his bungling and let him know it. They hissed and booed. Finally, the performer stepped downstage and appealed to the crowd. "Give me a break, folks. I don't write this crap."

Not even Shakespeare's brilliance can overcome a performer who adds nothing to the words. Any good performance is a blending of material and execution. That's especially true in comedy. You, the speaker, have to complement your material. You have to throw yourself into it.

The first syllable of "humor" is "you."

A speech is an interesting exchange. It's an intimate encounter between the speaker and the audience. A bond forms between them. An astute speaker encourages this relationship and takes advantage of it.

Carol Burnett was a good example of this. She was pleasant, friendly, and very down-to-earth in her opening question-and-answer session on *The Carol Burnett Show*. People gave her gifts, asked for kisses, told her that they knew old school chums of hers—you almost felt they were going to invite her over to the house for dinner after the show. Some of them may have.

Carol encouraged this chumminess. If someone wanted to come onstage to present a gift, or to give Carol a hug from her hometown, Carol waved her hand, saying, "Come on up." There were no bodyguards in evidence, like you'd see at an Elvis concert. These were friends. Backstage, though, we were sometimes nervous. A few of these "friends" didn't look too stable.

Carol, though, won the friendship and the trust of her audience. Now she could exploit it. I don't mean that in a demeaning way. It was nothing unethical or dishonest. I mean in a showmanship way. Now that Carol was a close friend, a buddy, she could dress up in the most bizarre, zany costumes and act silly. She could get away with more craziness because her audience loved her.

Others do it. Johnny Carson can get away with some slightly blue material because he's so well liked. He's clean-cut and honest-looking, therefore his raunchy jokes become just naughty. Red Skelton did the same before him. A nice man who ends every show with "God bless," wouldn't be doing anything inappropriate.

This device is not limited to show business personalities. People in other professions employ it too. No politician is a curmudgeon while campaigning. No, they love all the crowds, kiss all the babies, and eat whatever ethnic foods are presented to them. It's easier for them to sell their campaign promises to friends than to enemies.

Doctors and nurses call this "bedside manner," and it's tremendously important in their work. Winning the patient's friendship and trust makes the job they must do easier on them and on the patient.

For a speaker, we'll call it "podium-side" manner, and it means putting a little bit of yourself and your charisma into any humor that you attempt.

The Chinese translator in this chapter's opening anecdote had to do the stories just the way Bob Hope told them. He wasn't supposed to put himself into any of them; he was just to convert the stories from English to Chinese.

You have to put yourself into your stories. You can't do them word for word the way you heard or read them. If you wrote them, you naturally put a little bit of yourself into them already.

If a joke is good, though; if it made you laugh when you first read it; why can't you do it "as is"? Because the way you heard it or read it is the way that speaker or writer would do it; not the way you would do it. It would be awkward for you to do it verbatim and with all the same inflections. That's just not your style and the audience would sense it. They might not be able to verbalize it, but they would know something was wrong.

I told a joke to a group of speakers once—it's not a great story, but it illustrates a point. It went like this:

> I was doing a show one night and the couple at the front table were laughing, drinking, and having a good time. They were a great audience; I loved them, but I think they had a little too much to drink because the woman kind of slid right under the table, you know. She just disappeared from sight. So I interrupted my show, and said, "Excuse me, Sir, but your wife just slid under the table." He said, "Mind your own business. My wife just walked through that door."

One of the people in that group was a humorist. The following day he used that story, giving me credit, to illustrate comedy timing and delivery. He told the class, "Listen to the precise wording of the ending . . . 'That's my wife walking towards the table.'" Well, that wasn't the way I ended the story. Those weren't the words I used. Since he was using me as an example, I corrected him privately after the first seminar. He gave the seminar twice after that and still used his wording, not mine.

He had mentally converted that story to *his way of telling it*. In his mind, now, that was the correct wording and delivery. No matter how much I protested, he couldn't bring himself to offer his students anything less than the perfect way of telling the story.

That's commendable. It pissed me off, but it's commendable. This raconteur was so used to converting stories to his way of telling them that it became instinctive.

You must especially convert stories that you read. Writing is different from speaking. Literary style is not a conversational style. Even a good literary technique seems stilted in conversation. It has to be because the written page can't make gestures; it can't change inflection. Nuances have to be spelled out. When spoken, though, they're superfluous. If you say something in an angry tone, you needn't add, "He said angrily."

To illustrate, here's a golf story as it might be written. I'll tell the whole story, except for the punchline. I'll save that until I tell the story again in a more conversational mode.

Here's the story as written:

> One golfer was boasting to a playing partner about a new ball he had which he claimed was the greatest invention to ever hit golf. "If you hit this ball into the woods, it starts beeping," he said boastfully. "You can find it just by listening for the sound." His friend was impressed. "If you hit it in water, no problem. It glows. You look down, spot it, and scoop it out." His friend's eyebrows raised. Encouraged, the man continued. "If it gets buried in sand, this little antenna comes up so you can see it sticking out of the sand." The other player now was ecstatic. "That's great," he said. Now he wanted one. "Where'd you get it?" he asked. The first guy said . . .

With the proper gestures, facial takes, and voice inflections, a speaker would only need this much dialogue:

> I was playing golf and a guy was telling me about this great golf ball.
>
> He says, "This is the greatest golf ball in the world. Hit it in the woods, it starts beeping. You listen for the sound, you find it."
>
> He says, "Water? No problem. It glows. You look down, spot it, and scoop it out." I'm impressed.
>
> He tells me, "If it gets buried in the sand, this little antenna comes up so you can see it sticking out of the sand."
>
> I says, "Wow, that's great. Where'd you get it?"
>
> He says, "I found it."

You'll feel the difference even more if you say these two versions aloud.

Audiences are tolerant, too. They'll accept some stock jokes. They'll permit some "book" jokes. But they do expect you to do some work. If they notice that you're simply repeating the jokes as you saw them in a book, they'll be hurt. "Why should we sit and listen to you when we could cut out the middle man? We could read the book ourselves." And they're right. You at least owe them the courtesy of putting a little bit of yourself into the humor you offer them.

Of course, the material you write yourself reflects your point of view, your sense of humor, and your speaking style. At least, it should. But, material you gather from other sources should also have your trademark. How do you bend it to fit your own style? Here's how:

First, study any material that you gather to see how it might apply to you or your audience. Any joke or story has "essentials" and it has "accidentals." The essentials are those parts of the story or joke that are absolutely necessary for the humor. In Henny Youngman's trademark joke, "Take my wife . . . please," the "please" is absolutely essential. Without that, you have simply the cliché introductory statement, "Take my wife." That phrasing, also, is an essential. Why? Because it's the misdirection in the joke that sets up the surprise. "Take my wife" is an idiomatic statement meaning, "Let's change the subject to my wife." The switch is that Youngman takes the phrase literally. He's begging someone to take his wife away from him. But it's obvious that the gag wouldn't work if we used the translation instead of the figure of speech. "Let's change the subject to my wife . . . please" doesn't work.

The accidental in this case is "wife." We've all heard variations of this joke, because it's so famous that it's become part of our language. The original is the funniest, but these also qualify as humor:

A high school athlete saying at the awards banquet, "Now take our coach . . . please."

A speaker saying from the head table, "Now take this sweater I'm wearing," and his wife ad-libs from her seat on the dias, "Please."

To make a story yours, you need to analyze it and separate the essentials from the accidentals. Then you can change the accidentals to apply to you or your audience.

Devote some creative thought to this. If an anecdote begins with "These two guys went into a bar," examine it. Does it have to be two guys? Do they have to go into a bar? Can they go into the office cafeteria? Instead of any two guys, can it be you and the General Manager? Can it be the General Manager and the Vice-President from the main office? If the bar is an essential, can it be the bar that's across the street from the office—the one everyone knows about?

If a joke is about an umpire responding to a player's tirade, would it work just as well if it was about an inspector answering a factory worker? Could it be one spouse winning an argument against the other?

You get the picture.

A sales trainer talking to a group of stockbrokers told this story:

> I heard a very prominent scientist speaking one time and he asked if there was anyone in the audience with an I.Q. of over 170. A few hands went up and he said, "I'd like you to remain after this seminar. It would be nice to discuss the finer points of nuclear fusion with you." He then asked for I.Q.'s of over 150. When those hands went up, he invited them to remain, also. He said, "We could discuss relativity and its relation to national defense." Then he asked if there were any in the room with an I.Q. under 35. When those hands went up he said, "So, what do you think the market's gonna do?"

The joke is really a friendly put-down of the entire group. It catches them unawares. They don't realize which direction the speaker is headed in until he springs the punchline. Then they realize that he is saying, in effect, that anyone with an I.Q. of under 35 has to be a stockbroker. They know they've "been had" and they laugh.

How would you convert that joke to apply to your group? One way is to come up with a catch phrase that describes the group and throw it in as the punchline. For example, I might say to a group of television writers, "So, have you written any good pilots lately?" To a group of professional speakers, the same joke could end with, "So, about how many talks did you give last year?"

Another way would be to make the punchline apply to the "arch-rivals" of the group you're addressing. If you're talking to tennis players, the punchline applies to linesmen; if you're talking to personnel executives, the punchline applies to shop stewards; if you're talking to shop stewards, the punchline applies to personnel.

The secret is to extract the humor from any story and use it to relate to you and your listeners. It requires some creativity, and often much care. You don't want to destroy the comedy in the transformation process.

What happens, though, if you have a tale that simply won't permit itself to be changed—one that demands to be told as is? That's all right, because it's a story that you either read or heard. How and where you came across the story may be what relates it to you and your audience. If you're addressing a convention, you could have heard it at last year's convention. Maybe you heard two people discussing this as you checked into the hotel. It could be that your boss told this story to you in response to a question or complaint of yours.

In other words, the story may stay the same; your preamble personalizes it.

Purists may ask: "But what if I didn't hear it at last year's convention or as I came into the hotel or from my boss? Suppose my cousin from Cleveland told it to me over the phone?" Remember that this is humor. Its purpose is to enhance your primary message by entertaining your audience. This little chunk of your speech is meant to amuse; not to educate. A joke is not a history lesson. You're permitted poetic license if it improves your communication.

Another way to localize or personalize a story is to surround it with truth—truth about you or your listeners. Add local color to your story. This adds interest to the anecdote, and it adds credibility. The credibility helps the surprise of the humor. When you hear a speaker say, "That reminds me of a story," or "These two guys were walking down the street," you know a joke is coming. You wait for the punchline. It has to be good because the surprise element has been removed.

Listen to this, though: "Charlie and I were walking across the street to get a cup of coffee. We always stop for a coffee break around 10:30. That way we're back to the office in time for the 11 o'clock staff meeting." That sounds quite different from "These two guys were walking along the street," doesn't it?

A writing teacher used to drum that into us when I was in high school. Color adds excitement and credibility to your prose. He wouldn't let us just tell a story; we had to bring the reader into the story. They had to see what we saw; they had to feel the textures; they had to smell the aromas. I remember once he took points off a short story I wrote because I had a box of soap sitting on the washing machine. It should have been a box of Tide. The reader knew what a box of Tide looked like and could see it on top of the washer. A box of soap doesn't look like anything.

You, the raconteur, can do the same for your listeners. If your story begins with "two guys walking along the street," let your audience know which two guys. Tell them what street you're walking along, and why. Add detail that relates to this particular audience or to you.

I once sat with a famous entertainer and he told us about the time he was working with George Burns. He told us what theatre they were playing, why they were sitting backstage talking, what they were talking about, and lots of other specifics. He kidded George Burns about getting senile. George said, "No, I'm not senile. There are four sure signs of senility and I don't have any of them. First, you forget names, then you forget facts, then you forget to zip up." This entertainer then asked Burns, "What's the fourth sign?" George said, "You forget to zip down."

I loved that story because I felt like an insider. I was sitting in that dressing room kidding George Burns. I heard his off-the-cuff reply and laughed with these entertainers.

Then a few months ago I was researching an epigram for this book and read that exact quote attributed to someone else. The whole tale may have been apocryphal. Who cares? The point is that it had much more vitality when it was told to me as backstage banter, than it did as four lines of ink in a book of quotes. I enjoyed it more when I could see the ring of make-up on the collar of George Burns' robe. It was more memorable when it was told about people I knew, than it was as a lifeless one-liner in a book full of them.

By adding that flavor to your material, you can invigorate your stories for your listeners.

Now I know some reader is going to ask: "I have this story about playing a round of golf with this 1200-pound gorilla. How do I make that sound as if it really happened to me?" Unless you're addressing the National Association of Zoo Keepers and Caddies (NAZKC), it's difficult.

However, that doesn't mean you have to eliminate all the stories in your collection that are too bizarre to be believable. There are jokes about talking dogs, monkeys who stop in a bar for a drink, gorillas who play golf, cows who parachute—there are jokes about anything and everything. If they're funny, make a point, or fit into your presentation in any way, use them. You may have to sneak into them, though.

You can still analyze the story to find ways in which it applies to you or your audience. For instance, a gorilla playing golf is still a golf story. You play golf; the General Manager plays golf; probably most of the audience does.

Truth can be a big part of stories like these because they again add to the misdirection. This tale can have all the authenticity of a real golf challenge. You can name the course, give the details of the amount of money bet, and then bring out the gorilla.

It might help if you lead into the bizarre story with some easy little jokes along the way. That sets the spirit of fun. Then when you get to the gorilla, the audience knows it's been had. They've been hoodwinked. Now, they're willing to accept the goofiness of the story. It's similar to having met and talked with Carol Burnett as a real person at the opening of the show. After that, the audience was tolerant of the nuttiness of the sketches.

Let me illustrate with a story I used to tell about a friend of mine who was afraid to travel by air. No one believed the tale, but by the time they knew it was a fake, they didn't care. It went:

I had a friend—a fellow writer—who was afraid to fly. He was content to just sit in Hollywood and write for the TV shows. Then we got a great job offer to do a show in England.

Well, he was going to turn it down. He wouldn't fly. I said, "You gotta get rid of this fear. This is a big career move. It means lots of money. You can't turn it down just because you won't fly."

He finally called the airline. He said, "What's the chances of a bomb being on the plane with me?" The girl on the phone chuckled. She said, "Oh, about a million to one."

He didn't like those odds. He wasn't going. I argued with him; I reasoned with him. Finally, he got an idea and he called back the airline. He got the same woman. This time he asked, "What are the odds of two bombs being on the same plane with me?" Now she laughed out loud. She said, "That would be about 20 million to one."

Those odds he liked. Now he'll fly anywhere in the world. But he always carries one bomb with him.

Analyze, change, and rewrite any material that you do. Make it reflect you. Bring an audience into the story and let them be a part of it. Let them feel it as you tell it. Make them more than listeners; have them participate.

It does take a bit of effort, but it's worth it—for you and them.

Let me end this chapter with a couple of examples that show how to personalize and localize jokes. Take this simple joke:

I knew a golfer who was so dishonest he made a hole in one once and wrote down a zero.

Let's assume a paid speaker is working for a large organization. Mr. William White is a well-known executive on the association's board and is also a notoriously bad golfer. The speaker learned all this by questioning the program chairperson. The joke might be done like this:

I played golf with Bill White the other day. You have to do these things sometimes to get speaking engagements.

But I got a chance to know Bill pretty well. We had great conversations on each hole as we were trying to find our way back to the golf course.

Bill White is a reputable, trustworthy, honest business executive . . . until you put a golf club in his hand.

Then he CHEATS!

I'm telling you, I wouldn't make that accusation lightly. I'll give you an idea how bad he cheats at golf. On the 12th hole yesterday, he got a hole in one and wrote down a zero.

Here's another story that's been localized and personalized. Once again we're picking on poor Bill White.

I know that Bill White is in charge of this entire organization. He told me that several times himself, as I'm sure he tells you often.

Let me tell you, though, you're in competent hands with Bill at the controls. He takes care of your needs and I know he watches over your finances carefully.

You see, Bill invited me to breakfast at the coffee shop here at the hotel. I ordered the special, which was three eggs, any style, for $6.60. I had them scrambled.

Bill ordered the same thing. The waitress said, "Do you want yours scrambled?" Bill said, "No, M'am. Sunny side up. At $2.20 an egg, I want to count them."

Neither one of those stories ever happened. No one in the audience believed for a minute that they did. But for a moment at least, they did laugh at them. They relaxed, chuckled at the speaker (and at Bill), and then went back to the work at hand—listening to what the speaker wanted them to hear.

CHAPTER FIFTEEN

Some Humor Exercises:
(*Just to Prove You Can Do It*)

Using humor is work. It requires research, preparation, and practice. Some of the skills required are instinctive, but most are acquired. All of them can be developed or sharpened with practice.

This chapter lists twelve exercises you can do to help develop your comedic abilities, but you don't have to do them as one solid block. You don't have to start with exercise 1 and continue until you finish exercise 12. I would recommend doing them in that order in the first run through (In fact, some of them depend on you're having completed a previous example.), but after having completed them all, you can turn back and try any one or several of them again.

I heartily recommend that you use these exercises again and again. A proficient musician often returns to the scales, so we should return to the humor basics. Experiment with these exercises. Change them slightly, make them more fun. If possible, work with a few other people and make a game, a race, or a contest out of them. Somehow the competitive drive adds something to the practice of these exercises.

Another thing you might do to make these exercises pay off is to work on something that you can use in your speeches or in your work. For example, I once made an effort to research the greatest opening lines I had ever heard. It was good research practice, and I could then study the lines as a guide to my own speech openings. And, once I had them assembled, I wrote an article on them and sold it to a magazine.

I've used some of these exercises as gifts. People enjoy a book of personalized cartoons about themselves, or captions of old movie scenes with them as the star of the comedy (see exercises 9 and 10).

So use these initial exercises as a starting point and then get more creative. Change them, add to them, do them a little differently each time, but give them a try every once in a while. They'll keep you sharp.

Exercise 1:

This first drill is pure research. Find and save nine to twelve stories or one-line jokes that you like and that you might be able to use in your own communications.

You may approach this task any way you want. You could make it a must-get-done assignment, dig out a few magazines or books, and keep reading until you have the stories, or attack it in a leisurely manner. Simply be aware that you have to find usable humorous material and some lines will seem to jump out at you.

Naturally, the first approach is faster, but both have their benefits. If you want, you can convert this into exercise 1 and 1A. Do it both ways.

This exercise will accomplish a few things for you. First, it's good practice in research and gathering material. You'll find or become aware of new places to look for your stories.

Second, the jokes you select will tell you something about your sense of humor. You'll know a little more about the kind of comedy you like after you've gathered a dozen lines than you did before you started.

Third, you'll begin to sharpen your selective skills. There will be jokes you read that you reject. Either they're not funny enough or they're not right for you or your audience. That's an important judgment. Often it's not the jokes that speakers use that make them entertaining, it's the ones they have enough sense not to use.

Fourth, if you work this exercise periodically, you'll build up a repertoire. The first time you do it, save the material: you'll use it later in this chapter. In fact, save some of the material each time you do it. Paste the cut-out jokes into a looseleaf book, or retype them, or put them on index cards and file them. Use any system you choose, but keep them. They'll be a valuable reference for you.

Exercise 2:

This practice drill gets you using your memory as a resource guide. Come up with three stories that you might use in your speaking. They don't have to be finished or polished. The punchline may be weak or even missing totally—that's all right. You just have to find some incident that you feel can be useful in relating to your audience.

Get one story from your family, one from your work situation, and one from any other source. That last area could be a friend telling you about something that happened, it could be an incident that happened to you in traffic—anything besides the family or work.

These anecdotes, though, should be different from the ones you located in the previous exercise. Get these from your memory, not from a book or magazine. This exercise should show you the power of your recall. It should prove to you what a valuable resource your own history can be.

Let me give you an example of a story that I have filed away, but haven't used yet.

> My wife and I travelled from the West Coast to our hometown on the East Coast for a grade school reunion. Both of us attended the same parochial school, so we thought it would be a nice vacation and a chance to see some old childhood chums.
>
> The festivities began with an evening religious service. Since it began in a church, the guests were reverent enough to limit conversation. But as I glanced around at the attendees, I searched feverishly for one who might look older than I looked. I abandoned that and finally sought out one who just looked as old as I looked. I finally found him. He was about six pews ahead of me to the far left. I didn't know who he was. I couldn't remember him from school, but I was going to hang around with him a lot at the party.
>
> After the ceremony, the reunion began. I shook a few hands, hugged a few old girlfriends, but migrated toward the guy who looked my age. He stood next to a girl that I did remember from school. She remembered me, too. As I approached I got a big hug and kiss, then she took the arm

of the guy who looked my age and said to me, "Gene, you remember my Dad, don't you?"

Okay, have fun with this exercise. If you give it a little time and thought, you'll revive and enjoy stories that you thought you'd forgotten.

Exercise 3:

This research project will get you back to the reference books. The subject for this drill is "hard work." Later, when you do this again, you can substitute any topic you like.

Find a dozen good quotes, either humorous or ironic, that support your thoughts about hard work.

For instance, I can recall one off the top of my head that an athlete spoke when someone called him lucky. He said, "That's right, and it seems the harder I work, the luckier I get." If you run across that in your research, let me know who said it.

As an example of this exercise, I'm going to pick a different topic for myself. I don't want to give you an assignment and then do it for you. My subject will be "the value of humor."

Here are my dozen selections:

"We are all here for a spell, get all the good laughs you can."
Will Rogers

"In a comedy, laughs don't hurt."
David Picker

"Life does not cease to be funny when people die, any more than it ceases to be serious when people laugh."
George Bernard Shaw

"Laughter is the sensation of feeling good all over and showing it in one particular place.
Josh Billings

"It is a great misfortune neither to have enough wit to talk well nor enough judgment to be silent."
Jean De La Bruyere

"A satirist is a man who discovers unpleasant things about himself and then says them about other people."

Peter McArthur

"A person reveals his character by nothing so clearly as the joke he resents."

G.C. Lichtenberg

"Humor is laughing at what you haven't got when you ought to have it."

Langston Hughes

"Mark my words, when a society has to resort to the lavatory for its humor, the writing is on the wall."

Alan Bennett

"Nothing spoils a romance so much as a sense of humor in the woman—or the lack of it in the man."

Oscar Wilde

"A laugh is worth a hundred groans in any market."

Charles Lamb

"The most valuable sense of humor is the kind that enables a person to see instantly what it isn't safe to laugh at."

Anonymous

This exercise should give you some usable material. I know that one of these quotes will illustrate some point I'm making about humor. Another benefit of this exercise, and researching quotes, is that you get a good insight into what people are saying about the subject you're speaking about. Even though the quotes may not be usable, the ideas are. You may be able to springboard from a famous person's saying to a joke of your own that says it either better or funnier.

So have fun seeing what people said years ago to help you with next week's speech.

Exercise 4:

Now that we've tapped several resource areas to find some jokes, let's put them to use, or let's find a new one for a specific purpose.

In this exercise, create a piece of humor from any of your sources—an anecdote, quote, one-liner, whatever—that you can use as an opening line for a given situation.

The situation is this (and I purposely chose a unique one, so that you couldn't go to "the trunk"): You have been selected to christen a new luxury liner. Executives and employees of the shipbuilding company will attend the launching ceremonies. Your employers have been honored for the exhaustive work they've done for the shipbuilding company, and you've been selected to perform the honors because of your outstanding work for your company.

But along with this privilege comes responsibility. You must give a talk, and since you're representing your company—and a few of your executives will be there, also—you want to be good.

Try to find an opening that will be light-hearted and will capture the essence of this ceremony. Attack it from your point of view, your company's point of view, or the shipbuilding company's point of view. Heck, you can even attack it from the ship's point of view.

I'm sure you can top the line that I came up with when I wrote a short opening for a politician's wife who was selected for this same honor. She said:

"This is a privilege, but also a fun duty for me to perform. I think this will be the first time that I've ever hit anything with a bottle . . . that I wasn't married to."

Have fun with it.

Exercise 5:

Here is another mythical situation:

You are the boss who must announce to the employees that they are going to have to use a new system—it might be a new computer program, or a way of filing, whatever. It is a new system that they have been resisting. They much prefer the old way. They like the status quo. However, the higher-ups have opted for the change. It's up to you to make it palatable.

You need to come up with a humorous story, quote, or anecdote from any source, that will be a preamble to the statement you have to make. Your opening should illustrate the situation, tell the employees that they're going to change—whether they like it or not—and it will probably be for the good. (Refer to Chapter Ten. See the section on positioning humor to clarify or reinforce your salient points.)

Have fun with it.

Exercise 6:

This is the flip side of the previous exercise. In this drill you're going to make your point about a mythical situation, then you're going to reinforce what you've said with a bit of humor.

Let's assume that you introduced the new program from exercise 5. The people reluctantly got into the swing of things. The new system is now the modus operandi; it's accepted. However, many costly operator errors are now the problem. The workers either haven't taken the time to learn this new system properly or they're getting careless with it. Your message this time is to convince them that errors are costly, but they are also easily eliminated. You have to convince the workers to catch and correct errors before they become a problem.

Deliver that message, then find a piece of humor that reinforces your message and sets it in the listener's minds.

Have fun.

Exercise 7:

This exercise should teach you how flexible jokes can be. Take one of the jokes or stories you uncovered in exercise 1 or 2 and apply it in three different ways. In other words, try to find three morals for that one story.

Let me give you an example (actually three examples) of how I might apply the story that I used as an illustration in exercise 2:

1) You know, change is never pleasant. It's never easy to accept. Most of us would rather stay with the status quo. It's comfortable, we know it, there are few surprises. We like things like that because they rarely force us to postpone our coffee break.

But change is inevitable. It comes whether we like it or not. In fact, sometimes what we think is the "status quo" is actually change arriving more gradually.

I saw a great example of change not too long ago. My wife and I went home to an eighth grade reunion . . . *and so on.*

2) Maintenance is an important part of our job. We have to keep the tools and equipment in working order. It is part of our job and in a way it makes our work that much easier.

But it's an ongoing process. It requires constant care. As Jimmy Durante said at his 80th birthday party: "If I had known I was going to live this long, I would have taken better care of myself."

I know what Durante was talking about. Not too long ago my wife and I went home to an eighth grade reunion . . . *and so on.*

3) Image is an important part of any business. How the customer sees us. Sometimes that's not just how we look, but how we look in the customer's eyes.

I recently got a jolting lesson in how I must look in others' eyes. My wife and I went back home for an eighth grade reunion . . . *and so on.*

There are three different applications—morals—of the same story. Play with the anecdote or joke that you've selected. See if you can use that one piece of humor in at least three different ways.

Have fun with it.

Exercise 8:

Here, you'll learn to write simple little preambles into your anecdote. You'll notice in one of my examples from exercise 7, I threw in a Jimmy Durante quote. It's a funny line that helps set up the idea that I'm doing some humor at this point of my speech.

You'll also learn to write a few simple jokes of your own.

Using three of the stories that you uncovered in exercises 1 and 2, write a short preamble into each of them that incorporates three simple, build-up jokes. They needn't be long, they needn't be extraordinarily funny. They just have to show a touch of humor, of lightheartedness.

Here's an example, again of the story I used in exercise 2:

My wife and I just went home to an eighth grade reunion. It was a five-year reunion, of course.

No, actually it was a twenty-five year reunion. I was just lucky enough to graduate when I was six years old.

We thought it would be fun to see some of our old buddies and our old teachers. At first I was afraid to go. I still have homework I haven't completed.

But we went, and when we got there, I was sorry I did. I couldn't find anybody that looked as old as me. I searched and searched . . . *and so on.*

Just try that with some of your stories and I guarantee you'll surprise yourself.

It's not that difficult, so have fun with it.

Exercise 9:

You can have some fun with this drill and others can, too. Collect some clever cartoons from magazines or newspapers. Cut the caption off.

Then pick a theme. It could be about your work, your family, friends—anything at all. Now rewrite captions for the cartoons on that theme.

Try several captions for each cartoon. That gives you the luxury of selecting the best one.

I said others could have fun with this, because you can set up your work in book form and let people read it. It's great encouragement— seeing others laughing at your creativity.

This exercise teaches you how to write a punchline: a punchline is a kind of caption, too—a caption for a statement.

This is also a good exercise in learning how to analyze a situation and find the hidden humor. That's why you want to limit yourself to one theme—it forces you to keep searching for different angles. It makes you probe a little deeper for the more subtle ironies. If you do each joke on a different topic, it's too easy to select the most obvious idea.

Of course, later you can redo the exercise with various other themes. Have fun with it.

Exercise 10:

This drill is just like Exercise 9. All of the same rules and regulations apply except that instead of cartoons, you use photographs. You can collect old movie stills, baby pictures, or even photos from your own albums.

It's excellent practice in writing humor, analyzing situations, and thinking funny. It also can generate souvenirs that are worth keeping. Have fun with it.

Exercise 11:

Take any of the jokes or stories you've collected so far and change some of the elements to generate a new joke. Transform either the set-up or the punchline. Play with the story. Dissect it. Pull it apart and reassemble it to suit your needs.

I'll use my standard joke as an example again. I won't go through the set-up this time, I'll just go right to the punchline—and change it:

> "I went over to this girl I knew from grade school. In fact, I used to date her. I got a big hug and a kiss, then she said, 'It's great to see you again. Tell me, though, which one of your children did I go to school with?'"

Here's another version:

> " . . . then she said, 'I can't remember your name, but I do know you were always one of my favorite teachers.'"

You'll learn from this exercise that stories are not carved in stone. They can be altered. If you can learn to take some stories you like and adapt them to fit your situation, you can build up a usable repertoire quickly.

Exercise 12:

This last is a good exercise for learning to write your own humor without help from any other source. You just sit down to a blank sheet of paper, know what you want, think funny, then write.

To get started, though, you will build on outside help. Find a funny line that you like on the topic you want to work on, and then try to top that line. Write a better one. You can use the same idea that the original humorist used, but different wording. Or you can take an entirely different approach to the same problem.

Here's an example. I selected this line about meetings:

"Meetings: that's where people keep minutes, but waste hours."

Then I played with that concept:

"Meetings: that's where the executives keep minutes while their workers are outside wasting them."

"Executives love meetings. They discovered that talking about work was more fun than working."

"Our supervisors go to meetings three days a week. At these meetings, they're trying to figure out how come they're only getting two days' work out of us."

"If you added up all the work accomplished at meetings, you wouldn't have enough to hold a meeting over."

That's the idea. See if you can come up with five to ten lines on each joke that you try to top. It's great practice.

And remember, you can come back to these exercises at any time and try them over again. The more you do them, the more you'll learn.

PART III

Delivering Your Humor

"Seriousness is the only refuge of the shallow."
Oscar Wilde

CHAPTER SIXTEEN

Tips on Delivering Humor

Frustration dreams are common. Pilots dream of trying to take off from a runway that is littered with debris. Dancers dream that their legs become so heavy they can't lift them. A drummer dreams that when he hits the skin of the drum, it shatters. Perhaps these should rightly be called nightmares.

A speaker once told me of a frustrating dream she had. She arrived at the auditorium on the evening of her presentation, was introduced, walked onstage to whatever the singular of applause is, glanced into the auditorium, and saw that only one person was present. Speakers, even in their dreams, subscribe to the "show must go on" philosophy, so she began with her powerful opening. It didn't work. Not because the audience was so small, but because the audience—that one guy—wasn't paying any attention. He was reading something of his own.

After a few minutes speaking into a vacuum, the lecturer finally surrendered. "Look," she said to her audience, "this is a waste of my time and your time. Why don't we just call it a washout and both go back to our rooms?" The gentleman glanced up from his notes and said, "No, I'd rather you continue."

She did. You see, even in dreams, speakers know they don't get their fee unless they perform the service.

As it became more fruitless and more painful, she pleaded again with her listener. "Please continue," he insisted.

She endured through the entire speech, then said sarcastically, "I'm sure there are no questions." There were. The lone listener raised his hand continually, asking inane questions, which she graciously answered. He listened to none of her answers.

The frustration got to her, though. She shouted, "Why? Why do you force me to go on when you don't care what I'm saying. You're not even listening. Why must I continue?" The man said, "Because I'm the next speaker."

I don't believe she ever had that dream. You may not believe she ever told me that story. You're learning too many of my tricks from this book. The story, even if fabricated, makes a point, though. What is a speaker without an audience? It's like the sound of one hand clapping. No, better yet, it's like the proverbial tree that falls in the forest. It definitely makes noise, but no one is there to hear it.

Speaking is communication. It's an exchange of information; exchange is the key word. Someone offers and someone accepts. A speaker requires a listener, as we saw in the opening story—preferably more then one listener.

Humor is a specialized form of communication. It requires the humorist and someone to react to the humor. Audience reaction—whether belly laughs, chuckles, snickers, or smiles mixed with tears—is not spontaneous. That reaction must be orchestrated.

I once had a teacher—not a very inspiring instructor—who told the class flatly, "I don't care whether you learn this stuff or not."

He was right. It didn't affect his life. He offered information to us, told us what we should do to learn it, then withdrew from the process. The rest was up to us. If we learned it, we gained; he neither gained nor lost. If we ignored it, we lost; he neither gained nor lost. He was completely disinterested.

You can be that kind of speaker, if you like. You can prepare your discourse well, present it clearly, and then fold up your notes and leave the podium. Each listener is free to take notes, analyze them, study them, and gain what they want from your lecture.

Speakers can be like that; humorists can't. (And, for those parts of your speech where you present humor, you are, in effect, a humorist.) Humor demands a return from the audience. Without laughter—or an appropriate response of some kind—a humorist is one hand clapping. You can't be dispassionate.

If that teacher I told you about had been paid according to the grades of his students, he would have been very concerned about our learning. He would have forced homework and study on us because he would have had something to gain or lose. In presenting humor, you will always have a stake in how your audience receives it. Not a financial interest; an emotional one. If you're going to do a joke, you want to get a laugh.

If you want something from your audience, you must give to your audience. You can't expect to get laughs; you must earn laughs.

Till now in this book you've been "getting ready" to present humor. You've gathered material, analyzed it, rewritten it. Eventually, you have to face the mike. Some speaker introductions seem endless, but they're not. They do end. When they end with your name you have to stand up and speak.

But not yet—at least, not yet as far as this book is concerned. You still have some preparatory work to do. You need to polish your delivery.

Sometimes an outstanding performer can salvage mediocre material. A bad performance, though, can destroy even the most superb writing. You've worked hard at assembling your humorous material. Since you're the performer, you owe it to you—the author—to be excellent.

These tips should help:

Know you can perform the material: I've worked with many talented, legendary performers—Bob Hope, Carol Burnett, Phyllis Diller, Sammy Davis, and others. They're all limited. Everyone is. Don't misunderstand (and I hope they don't)—their talent is stupendous. They do what they do splendidly. But they do what they do.

The reason they are so successful is because they know their limitations. Professionally, they perform only what they know they can do and can do well.

The rest of us aren't always so smart. We attempt things that we think we should be able to do. We should only try what we *know* we can do. Often our minds or our egos are to blame. Someone explained that Bing Crosby's popularity was due to the fact that most people, in the shower, thought they sang like him. In their heads they did, but a tape recorder would have shown them to be wrong. That's our egos deceiving us. Egos tell some of us that we're as inventive as Robin Williams. Getting no laughs from friends at the party doesn't deter us. Ego tells us that we're funny—contrary opinions be damned!

There is some humorous material that we can't or shouldn't do. Like the professionals, we have to learn our limitations.

Suppose, for example, you have a piece of material that demands a Humphrey Bogart impersonation. It's a funny bit, but it must have a Humphrey Bogart sound-alike. You can tell that joke in your mind and be superb. In your own head you sound exactly like Bogie. However, when you try to tell it aloud, you sound like you're doing an impression of Edward G. Robinson, or maybe Woody Allen, perhaps Joan Rivers, or even Lee Iacocca. Whoever you're doing, it ain't Bogart.

Impersonations are a talent unto themselves. There are other jokes that you may not be able to do. I once auditioned actresses for a role in which they had to scream—and scream convincingly. It sounds simple, but many people can't scream at the top of their lungs. They try, but the sound that comes out is half scream and half apology. Try it yourself sometime and see if you're honestly convincing.

I'm one of the non-screamers. I find it difficult doing any stories that are too loud. I feel uncomfortable, and the audience is never convinced. Here's a story I can't tell:

> A man was explaining how he bagged the lion head trophy that is mounted on his wall. He said to a friend, "I was tip-toeing through the thick underbrush. We knew there was game in the area, but we weren't sure exactly where it was, nor how close. Suddenly, the bushes in front of me parted. This huge cat poked his head through and roared—ROOOAAARRRR!!! Unfortunately, I wet my trousers." The friend said, "I don't blame you in the least. I would have, too." The man said, "No, not then. Just now when I went ROOOAAARRRR!!!"

It's a good story and fun to tell, but I can't do it well. To tell that story effectively, you have to roar loudly—loudly enough to convince an audience that you might wet your trousers. When I roar, it's unconvincing. So I don't tell the story.

Dialects, if they're a part of the story, are another area where people think they sound exactly right, but often don't.

How do you know if you can tell a story effectively? Try it. Say it aloud. It does no good to rehearse it in your head, because in our heads we all sound talented. Say it out loud and honestly evaluate the results. If you can tell it, fine; if you can't, replace it.

Rehearse your humor: If you have a story or bit of humor that you can deliver, now you have to learn to deliver it well. You learn that through practice—through rehearsal.

I still remember the first monologue I delivered in public. It was at a party for my supervisor who was retiring. I wrote a 35-joke routine about him, and rehearsed it every night for a month. I practiced that speech so much that once I started the first joke I couldn't stop until I got to the last one. It became like one long sentence.

Still this was my first try at comedy, so I didn't trust myself. I had the speech in my hand as I spoke, and it went well. The audience was receptive. They laughed; my supervisor roared; and I was hooked on comedy.

A friend complimented me afterwards, saying, "Congratulations, that was a great talk. But tell me something. How could you read that paper with your hands shaking so much?"

I probably couldn't have read it. I had the speech memorized from having recited it so often. As I mentioned, once I started that opening joke, the rest of the jokes just fell out. I couldn't have stopped them if I wanted. The point is that even though I was physically trembling (and I was), my voice didn't falter. I didn't "phumpher" any of the words. Why? Because the rehearsal paid off.

Again our minds can trick us. We have a humorous routine that we know very well. We feel safe with it. However, when we get before the crowd, we can lose it. We forget key words, or suddenly find we can't pronounce them. "Good evening" comes out of our lips as "Geebning."

The only protection is rehearsal.

Now It's Time for You to Speak

At last, the introduction is completed and you step to the microphone—to try your humor. As this book advised earlier, jokes aren't the only form of comedy. Your humor can be an attitude, a gesture, a certain voice inflection, a glance—almost anything. However, since everyone will be doing something different, and since most humor involves story or joke-telling, here are a few tips on telling a joke. Most of them also apply to other styles of humor.

1. Understand your humor: Earlier I told you about a mean joke I pulled on one of my high school classmates. I told a meaningless joke to several accomplices who laughed uproariously at it. All of us were in on the deception except the hapless victim, who laughed when we did. Most people would. We laughed so hard at him that he thought the joke must be funny and he laughed harder. He had no idea what the punchline meant, but he was doubled up laughing. The real payoff came later, as we heard our victim retelling the "joke."

Many of us do that. We hear a joke get laughs. We don't quite understand it, but assume it's funny because other people are laughing. You really can't do justice to a story that way. Why? Because you don't know how to tell it. You don't know what to emphasize. You don't know what expressions or voice inflections to use. You don't know what you're talking about.

I sometimes chuckle to myself when I hear television actors reciting technical medical terms. They're trying to act, but they have no idea what they're saying. "I hate to tell you this, Sarah, but your husband's diaphoresis may be symptomatic of ischemial infarction. We won't know until the pylograms are interpreted by the renologists." How can the actor say that as if he means it when he has no idea what it means? (I just wrote it, and I have no idea what it means.)

Good performers find out what it means. They ask the writer, the director, the producer, fellow actors. Chances are none of them know, either. If not, they'll call a medical doctor and have him reduce the medical mumbo-jumbo to understandable laymen's terms. The point is to know what you're saying before you say it.

Once we had a guest on a variety show. In a sketch about a French restaurant, the writers wrote in a few French words as the order. When the guest, who spoke French, read the script, she went into a fit of laughing. She asked permission to ad-lib her order and we naturally allowed it. What the writers had her requesting as a gourmet meal was "All the bread you want and a glass of meat."

Before telling a joke or story, you should first know that it's funny, believe that it's funny, and know why it's funny. That doesn't mean you should be able to sit someone down and do a treatise on the humor of the given story. No. It's difficult to reduce comedy to an analytical explanation. Someone said it's like dissecting a frog. You may learn something, but you kill the creature in the process.

But you should have a feeling for the humor. Not necessarily a feeling that can be verbalized, but an internal knowledge that you enjoyed the story and there is a logical reason why you did.

2. Know the punchline: This part of the book probably should have been printed in red. If there is any one section that will help people use humor effectively and effortlessly, it is this one. *Know and understand your punchline.*

As a young writer, I heard the producer of a variety show give his staff some advice. To me, it was stupid. It was so obvious and basic that I thought it was dumb even to mention it to a group of professional comedy writers. He said, "You've got to tell the audience when to laugh." I laughed at his advice.

Later I learned it was very solid and useful advice. Comedy, especially professional comedy, is supposed to make people laugh. You can't depend on an audience laughing as one without a cue. You have to tell them when to laugh.

I know this is confusing, so let me illustrate. Suppose you have a trained dog act on stage. The trainer calls the dog toward her with enthusiasm and confidence. The dog never moves. That can be funny, but there is no laugh trigger. Does the crowd laugh as soon as the trainer calls the dog? Probably not. They'll just assume that the animal takes some time to respond. Then do they laugh after five seconds? Maybe. How about after ten seconds? They may be bored with the bit by then and not bother to laugh.

Then how do you trigger the reaction? How do you let the audience know when to laugh? The trainer will do that. She'll call the dog and get no response. Some people might laugh there. After a pause the trainer will look sadly to the audience. Aha! Now they know it's a comedy bit. Now they have permission to laugh.

The trainer can then call the dog again, with a comic punchline. "Come on, girl. It's only an hour show, girl." The audience knows to laugh again.

The point is that in the telling of a joke or story, in trying to get a laugh of any kind, you have to know what the laugh is and where the laugh is. Then you provide the leadership. You tell the audience when to laugh.

Remember, humor is like mentally pulling the rug out from under your listeners. You trick them. You lead them to a certain spot on the rug, you make them feel secure there, then you tug on the rug and send them tumbling. That requires timing.

If they know you're going to pull the rug out from under them, they won't get on it. They won't be tricked. Even if they do get on, and you tip your hand too soon, they'll abandon the rug. You'll be left with a handful of carpet and no joke.

The same is true with humor. The punchline is the trick, the gimmick. Everything leads to that. If it doesn't, you destroy the effect.

When you know your punchline and fully understand the effect that punchline will have, you can then channel everything you say and do—gestures, words, inflections—towards that end.

Abbott and Costello used to do a routine in their movies that illustrates what happens when you don't fully understand the punchline.

Bud Abbott said to the comic, Costello, "Have you ever ridden a jackass?" Costello said, "No." Bud Abbott said, "Well, you'd better get onto yourself."

Later Costello tried to use the same joke on one of the heavies in the film. He said, "Have you ever ridden a jackass?" The guy said, "No." Costello turned around and said, "Hop on, I'll give you a ride."

Know where you're going with each bit of humor you use. Understand the joke and know where the laugh is. Keep the laugh in mind throughout the telling. That will guarantee that everything you say and do builds to that punchline.

3. Tell the story economically: Humor has an economic logic to it. Listeners will invest their time if the humor is worth it. Occasionally they'll get a bargain. They don't want to overpay for a punchline, though. Your best bet as the storyteller is to give them good value. As they say in the commercials, "Give them the lowest prices in town."

Each one of your punchlines needs a setup. You can't have humor without a certain amount of "pipe-laying." But keep the setup concise. Get to the point quickly. Certainly, don't cut the build-up so much that you confuse the punchline. You need to figure out what information you must give for the joke to be understood. Give all the necessary details with enthusiasm and energy, but give them efficiently. Deliver the punch and move on. Don't turn a simple anecdote into a shaggy dog tale.

Suppose, though, you have a tale that requires a long setup. Fine. Do it. That's part of the economy of the joke. However, be sure that the story is worth it. Otherwise, you'll get groans instead of laughs.

One way to tell a longer story and keep the audience satisfied is to add some bonuses along the way. Add a few chuckles to the long buildup. This way the listeners don't feel as if they're "paying" for just the punchline. They're also "paying" for the extras.

Some comics take a simple joke and turn it into a routine. Flip Wilson used to do that. He'd tell one story for eight to ten minutes. When comedians do that, they add punchlines along the way. It's only one story, but it's a series of punchlines.

One word of advice: if you have a good story that doesn't seem to be working, the first place to look for improvement is in the length. Shorten it. Tell it more succinctly. If you get it down to its bare minimum and it's still not working, perhaps you should look for a new piece.

4. Tell your story slowly: One drawback to knowing your story well—knowing why it's funny, knowing where the laugh is, and rehearsing it—is that you often get to know your story too well. Each word is set in your own mind. You know the story works and will get laughs so you can't wait to get to the best part—the punchline.

Many humorists tell their best stories so quickly that they're almost unintelligible. They're like doctors writing a prescription. The medical advice is expert, but only a pharmacist can interpret it—maybe.

Of course, the punchline is the reason for telling the story. It's the cue for the audience to laugh. But, it loses much of its effectiveness if folks have to pause and wonder what you said. They might have an idea, but if they have to supply the syllables they didn't quite hear, they're not going to laugh. It's like doing a jigsaw puzzle with a few pieces missing.

It reminds me of the bit Woody Allen devised with the hold-up note in *Take the Money and Run*. He handed a note to the teller who read, "Give me all your money. I have a gub." She asked, "What's a 'gub?'" Allen said, "It should say 'gun.'" She insisted it read, "gub."

What good is a hold-up note that can't be read? What good is a joke that can't be heard? Take your time and let people hear every word of your brilliance.

5. Be aware of your listeners: Which is a good joke and which is bad? Nobody can tell you that except the audience. The writers, the comedians, the professionals, are all only guessing. It may be an educated guess based on experience, but it is a guess. Everyone in the profession has seen a gag work fantastically one evening only to sit there laughless the next. Why did the first audience react while the second didn't? Who knows? Each audience a performer faces seems to say, "You tell the jokes; we'll decide what's funny."

Whether you as a humorist like it or not, the audience becomes a partner in each of your stories—you would prefer they not be silent partners, of course. They are a part of your humor and can't be ignored.

Be aware of your partners, your listeners. We all are, sometimes. "I don't want to tell this story in mixed company." In effect, you're saying that certain people here won't appreciate this joke, therefore I won't tell it. That's commendable (even if the joke may not be).

Respect your audience. Don't give them stories they don't want to hear. For instance, I have a joke about an ugly tie that my children gave me one Father's Day. I tell the audience I wear the tie because I don't want to hurt their feelings, but I usually wear it to candlelit dinners. "For two reasons," I explain. "It's darker, and I hope the damn thing catches fire." It's a harmless gag, but at church functions "damn" becomes "dumb."

Should you tell off-color stories? Ethnic jokes? That's your call, but your audience should have a vote, too. If they don't want them, don't tell them.

How do you know? First, be aware of who your audience is. Hear your humor as they would hear it. Analyze it from their point of view. If you were sitting out there listening, would you be offended?

You can ask, too. Check with someone who should know. "Would this story offend this audience?" "Would you prefer that I changed this word?" Responsible people will be honest with you because they want a good speech from you.

Remember, you're using humor to enhance your message. If your humor offends, it interferes with what you have to say. It's not worth it. If in doubt, drop it.

6. Leave the laughing to your audience: When you do humor, you're performing. You're entertaining. You become an actor. You have to tell your tale full out, with conviction. Say it and mean it.

I remember Carol Burnett giving some advice to a fine dramatic actor who guested on her show. This person was not used to comedy and tended to laugh when he did or said something funny. Carol said, "When you're angry at me, be angry." In other words, the audience has no fun if the performer is having fun when he or she is supposed to be enraged. If the rage is necessary for the humor, then there should be fierceness in the voice, not a chuckle.

In *The Odd Couple*, Walter Matthau chased Jack Lemmon onto the roof of their apartment building and berated him for being an intolerable roommate. After a vicious harangue from Matthau, Lemmon said, "You want me out of the apartment, is that sort of what you mean?" Matthau glared at him and screamed, "No. That's *exactly* what I mean."

It was a brilliantly funny line, but Matthau the actor couldn't share in the fun. He had to be furious when he delivered it. That was the only way the rest of us could enjoy it. Without that wrath, there was no fun.

You have to be the story teller; not the listener. You have to act out the story; not enjoy the humor of it at the same time.

If you tell an angry story, be angry. If you're confused, act confused. Be whatever the story demands. Don't laugh as you set the story up and don't laugh as you do the punchline—unless, of course, that's a part of the telling.

There are exceptions, naturally—there are to everything. But for the most part, act out your playlet and leave the enjoyment of it to the audience.

"Wait a minute," you say, "Some pretty funny people laugh at their own jokes. It doesn't hurt a bit." I agree. I'm not saying that you can't laugh on stage, or enjoy your own humor along with the listeners. However, tell the story first, and then you can realize, along with the audience, how funny it truly was. Laugh as much as you want at that point.

Don't let your laughter, though, destroy the telling of the tale. Don't let your fun interfere with the audience's fun.

7. Let your humor speak for itself: I'm a professional writer-humorist. I would love to have a scathing comeback for those people who say to me, "Say something funny." Apparently, I'm not a clever enough writer-humorist to pen my own witty response to that request. Usually, I say, "Not for free," or "This is my day off."

But it's a demanding challenge to meet: "Say something funny." I don't need that kind of pressure.

You don't have to create that kind of pressure for yourself, either. When your preamble to a story is, "Here's a great joke," you have to deliver a "great joke." You put an unnecessary burden on your punchline.

Your story may be "great," and you may know it's "great." It's always been "great" before, and it will be "great" this time, too. Fine, but let the audience discover that.

Most good tales don't need a preamble. You usually don't have to introduce good stories. Get to them; the audience will pick up the connection of that humor to your message.

If your story absolutely requires an introduction, avoid superlatives. Let the praise come from the listeners in the form of big laughs.

Does all of this guarantee that every joke you tell is going to work? No. Remember, only the audience knows what's funny. You and I are only guessing.

Are some of your jokes going to miss by a little bit? Are some going to get chuckles where you wanted guffaws? Are some of them going to go over like the proverbial lead balloon? Yeah. What do you do then? That's the next chapter.

CHAPTER SEVENTEEN

How Do I Know the Jokes Will Work?

This is the beginning of my speech when I give a talk near my own neighborhood:

> "Thank you very much. You know, it's nice to work so close to my own hometown. I don't know whether you know it or not, but I can leave this auditorium, hop in my car, and be back inside my own home in less than five minutes. Now that may not mean much to you, but with the talk I give, to me it can be a lifesaver."

That's only a joke. (Most of the time it's a joke, anyway.) It's a joke, though that reflects a real concern of most speakers. That's the question that people ask most when I lecture to business or professional speakers on comedy: "What do you do if the jokes don't work? My usual, cocky response is, "If that ever happens to me, I'll get back to you."

The arrogance of that flippant reply usually gets a laugh, but it does convey the essence of the answer. Proper preparation is the warranty you're searching for against failure. Do everything that you have to do to guarantee that the jokes won't fail, and surprisingly, most of them won't.

As a comedy writer, I'm sometimes annoyed at the analysis, rewriting, and changing required of some of the scripts that we work with. We study each word of the draft. We spend hours improving just one joke. Enough, already. Why must we put that much effort into polishing an acceptable script?

I got my answer when we were preparing a monologue to be done at a command performance celebrating the 25th anniversary of the coronation of Queen Elizabeth. Bob Hope was running through the cue cards backstage at the Palladium. I sat next to him as he was giving the routine one last look-see.

He dropped one line. Before they could remove the cue card, though, I protested. It was my joke. "Bob," I said, "Why are you taking that joke out?"

"It's not funny." He said. "The Queen won't laugh at that."

I answered, "It's a funny joke. The Queen will love it." (Like I know Queen Elizabeth's taste in humor.)

Hope said, "Will she really?"

I said, "Sure."

He took the cue cards, handed them to me, and said, "Then you do it."

He followed the advice I've given often in this book: When in doubt, cut it.

He had worked hard on this monologue, which would be performed before royalty and seen by millions of viewers on international television. He didn't want to have to wonder, "What do I do if the jokes don't work?"

The first step in safeguarding the effectiveness of your humor is to do the preparatory work. Do everything we've talked about in this volume so far. Work on your material with energy and enthusiasm. Put as much work into your comedy relief as you put into the primary message. It's an investment in your message.

Besides, if you're going to do humor, you want to do it well.

Going back to our example from the Palladium in London, can we assume that all of the monologue jokes were fabulous laugh-getters? No. Some were giant laughs; some were fair; some were disappointments. There might even have been a bomb or two in there.

Then what's the point of all the preparation, polishing, and rewriting, if it still can't guarantee the success of each joke?

We have to take a look at the nature of comedy. Johnny Carson kids often about the "peaks and valleys." He usually mentions it when he's in one of the valleys. It's true. A comedy monologue builds to a crescendo of laughter, trails off, then begins building again. You must have high points and low points. Why? Because many jokes suffer in comparison to other jokes.

I once wrote and produced a variety show for Tim Conway. Tim had been cancelled so many times that his personalized license plate read "13 WKS." That represents the 13 weeks he was on the air before the network decided another show might do better in that time slot. My partner and I were determined to make this a funny, interesting variety show that would get Tim Conway renewed.

After the taping of the premier show, we felt we succeeded. It was a good show. Practically everyone happily congratulated us. Then one of the network executives offered his critique: "You know what was wrong with this show? Some parts of it were funnier than others." This was from one of the intellects who would decide whether this show would be renewed for a second 13 weeks.

I said, "That's our fault. We tried to make them all have the same degree of funniness."

There is no way that a series of jokes in a monologue or sketches in a variety show can be equal. Some have to get bigger laughs than others, and they should. If they were all the same, the result would be monotonous. The bigger laughs add excitement; the smaller laughs set up the bigger laughs. It's Carson's proverbial peaks and valleys.

The same applies to some of the humor that you add to your speech. Maybe the section at the beginning works well, but the routine doesn't get the giant laughs you expected later on. Maybe the ending is powerful, but the bit before it is only fair. None of this spells failure.

Judge your humor by the overall effect. Does it enhance your message? Does it get your audience to listen? Does it prompt them to respect you? Does it help them remember what you say?

This is not to say that you should accept the weaker portions and be content with them. No—try to make them better.

We writers once had an assignment to write special lyrics for a song. There were about 11 places in the song for humor—spots where the music stopped and the comic did a few jokes. We had struggled with this material for about two years.

Finally, the performer called and said that he was happy with all of the material except one joke. It just wasn't working. I called the writers together and said, "Let's write the greatest joke in the world. Let's make this guy happy so we can get rid of this thing once and for all." We did. We worked and reworked until we came up with a selection of about five or six terrific gags.

We sent them off and the next day I received a phone call from our client. "Those new jokes you sent me were fantastic," he said. "I put them into the act last night and they got screams." I couldn't wait to call the other writers to give them the good word. Then the comic added, "You know something, though. They're so funny they make the other jokes look bad. Work on them."

You can always improve the weaker material, but don't be too hard on yourself. Don't surrender because some parts of your routine are less effective than others.

Every baseball player would love to get a hit each time at the plate. Would he settle for a hit every third time at bat? Most would be delighted with a .333 average.

And every batter is going to strike out once in a while. Everyone who attempts humor is going to "bomb." It's not that big a deal, if you can keep your average respectable.

Be careful, though. Ball players hit at a .333 average because they work at it. They take batting practice, watch for defects in their swing, and correct them. They step up to the plate looking for a hit every time. If they relax and say, "I'll only try for a hit every third time to the plate," they'll wind up hitting safely in only one out of each nine tries—or less. Instead of batting .333, they're taking a .111 batting average back to the minor leagues.

Go for the big reaction with all your humor. Be determined to score big each time, but not disappointed when you don't.

Why do speakers ask that one question over and over: "What do you do if the jokes don't work?" It's because professional comics, with their high visibility, have frightened us. "I bombed." "I died." "I stank." Those are all graphic, unpleasant verbs that describe failed humor.

We have to remember that comics are usually insecure people. They worry about their careers. They fret over how much they're loved. They exaggerate. Of course, they have more reason to worry than we have. They earn their livelihood and they earn the audience respect they crave through their humor. If they're not funny, they're not making a living.

But, no business speaker has ever been lynched by an audience angered by an anecdote that bombed.

At best, that anecdote can help your message immeasurably. At its worst—when it bombs, dies, or stinks—it does very little harm. It does very little harm, that is, if used sparingly.

Don't overload your presentation with comedy. Remember, a little cayenne pepper can add character and zest to your chili recipe. Dump in the whole container and you may have to serve fire extinguishers instead of finger bowls. You don't want to be a humorist with a message; you want to deliver a message with a touch of humor.

Too much humor increases your risks without paying proportionate dividends. Fail once and the audience is forgiving; fail a few times and they're disappointed; fail a lot and they begin to suspect both message and message bearer.

Nevertheless, even with dedicated preparation, the correct amount of humor, and polished delivery, jokes still fail. That's never fun. What do you do when you "flop?"

It helps to take it in stride. I once watched George Burns taping a television special. He caused some turmoil when he blew a line. The director had to stop the action; the cameras had to reposition; and the actors had to go back a few pages in the script. George remained calm, looked out into the audience and said, "I'm an old man. What do you expect?"

The audience laughed, applauded, and loved him for it.

Tony Randall is another old pro who has fun with his mistakes. He prepares for possible flubs. He often tells the studio audience before taping begins, "They call me 'One-Take Tony.' I've been in the business over 50 years, and I've never made a mistake during a taping. I don't take any credit for it; it's just luck, I suppose." Then if and when he does blow a line, everyone has fun with it and forgives him.

Dean Martin on his televised variety show would often leave mistakes in the tape. It was part of his mystique. The audience loved it because watching his show was like watching "live" television. Anything might happen at any time and if it did, Dean Martin didn't care. He'd let you see it. He had nothing to hide.

On the other hand, Shelley Berman, was at the peak of his career when a televised documentary showed him losing his cool. While he was performing onstage, a backstage telephone rang. The TV cameras showed his fury when he came offstage. He ranted at everyone in sight and pulled the phone out of the wall. He behaved like a maniac and America didn't like it. His career tailed off after that and many feel that telecast was the reason.

The message to you and me is: "Don't fall apart when your humor does." Keep your sense of humor, which means you shouldn't take the incident too seriously. Remember a sense of humor is the ability to see, recognize, and accept the reality of any occurrence. That's what you need to do here—keep the failure of one chunk of comedy in perspective.

The following thoughts may help you do that:

1. The 'tragedy' is usually magnified: That ill-timed phone call disturbed Shelley Berman much more than it did the audience. "It destroyed the entire mood of the piece," he claimed. "It ruined my entire performance." It didn't.

In Mr. Berman's defense, the documentary distorted the actual happening. That backstage phone rang once before, at a less critical part of his act. He joked the interruption away and continued his act. Afterwards he asked the backstage workers to disconnect the phone during his performance. They forgot. Then when it rang a few days later at a critical part of his dramatic finish, he blew his cool. The documentary implied that these incidents happened in reverse order— he blew his stack first and then joked the incident away later.

Regardless, neither incident was that momentous. The audience would have tolerated both interruptions. Mr. Berman, though, abandoned logic and reason when the second one occurred. The reality of the events didn't justify his reaction.

If you can keep your sense of humor and at least postpone any over-reaction, you'll usually find on reflection that the "tragedy" was no tragedy after all.

2. The "tragedy" is more painful to us than it is to our audience: When we tell a bad joke or an anecdote that doesn't work, we're embarrassed. We feel we've made fools of ourselves before an auditorium filled with people. Someone once convinced me that embarrassment is a reverse form of ego. If we have a slight stain on our tie, we think the entire world will notice. We feel we're so important that every stranger we pass on the street will inspect our tie and condemn us for that blotch. If we tell one joke in our speech that doesn't work, we immediately project that this crowd will do nothing else all day except discuss among themselves how badly this one story fared. We are frightened, panicked, terrorized. Our concentration can be affected throughout the remainder of the program.

Chances are that hardly anyone noticed. If they did, the failure wasn't as momentous as we thought. Even if it was, probably no one will take it out of the auditorium. They have more important things scheduled for the rest of their day.

A dumb incident once showed me how little others really notice us. A fellow I was working with agonized over shaving his beard. He was tired of it and it was bothering him. Yet he felt it was a part of his personality, a feature that all of us had grown attached to. Was it fair for him to decide arbitrarily to shave it off?

Well, he did. None of us noticed. We worked with him all morning and never commented on his naked face. (Well, almost naked—he kept the moustache.) We honestly never missed the beard.

When we went to lunch, he confessed that he was offended. He felt like the wife whose husband didn't compliment her new dress.

We lunched at our usual cafe. We had been eating there for over a year. We knew everyone and everyone knew us. As soon as we walked in, we presented our newly shaven friend to our waitress. We said, "Do you notice anything different about Barry?" She didn't. We urged her to look closely. Still nothing. We prompted her to look closely at his face. Now she sparked. Her eyes lit up and she said, "Oh, sure. You've grown a moustache."

People don't analyze us as much as we think they do. They won't analyze your humor as much as it seems when you're on the podium, either.

Any glitches in your routine will be more painful to you than they will be to your listeners.

3. The audience is rooting for you: A speaker and an audience are not adversaries. There may be a touch of the love-hate syndrome, but generally the audience is on the speaker's side. Why shouldn't they be? They have to be there to listen. It makes sense that they would want you to be entertaining.

An occasional disappointment in your presentation won't turn them against you. Falter slightly and they'll rush to your support.

The only way they might abandon you is if you force them into it. Try to blame them for your problems, and you'll polarize them against you. If you blame yourself, though, you'll have a roomful of supporters.

That's why I'm uncomfortable with speakers who focus on the negative—even if they're justified. I've seen lecturers with bad microphones who remind the audience of it every two or three minutes. I've seen performances where a light flickered. The speaker wouldn't allow the audience to ignore it. She kept mentioning it throughout her stay on stage.

This is a strictly parenthetical suggestion, but in a sense it ties in with humor that fails. If anything goes wrong with your presentation, whether it's your fault or the promoter's fault, work through it. You might mention it, and perhaps ad-lib about it, but then forget it. Continual reminders distract from your message and your effectiveness. Anyone should be able to give a speech under ideal conditions. All of us, though, must be able to work under flawed conditions.

In most cases, if you're honest and have a sense of humor, the audience will be supportive.

One friendly warning, though: If you do ad-lib, keep the comedy aimed at yourself. Caustic comments directed towards the audience, the promoters, or anyone else can be offensive. You may run into the same kind of disapproval that Shelley Berman did. It's much safer to make yourself the brunt of your comments.

At a banquet talk I gave, a ceiling light fixture flickered a few times and went out. An ad-lib could have kidded the hotel about not paying its electric bill. I might have kidded the host association about only booking the room till a certain hour. But these could have been misinterpreted. Instead I said, "I've often had people doze off during my talk, but never an entire chandelier."

4. The audience will enjoy your frustration (if you do): Carson nightly turns his "bombs" into "blockbusters" by kidding about them. Some people even feel that he plants one or two "clinkers" into his monologue so that he can joke about them.

The most fun I ever had at a lecture was one time when I could hardly deliver the talk. The room next door featured a piano player and an opera singer. We only heard the highest notes of the performance, but they seemed to come at the most inopportune times. We—the audience and I—enjoyed it. We laughed at the situation together. I laughed so hard that when things finally quieted down, I could hardly speak.

People like those gaffes. That's why the rash of blooper shows we had on TV were so popular. Folks like to be "in" when things go wrong.

Your gaffes may turn into gems if you allow the audience to see them and be a part of them. Have fun with them as Carson does. They may turn out to be not only less painful, but a big plus for your presentation.

So far, though, I'll admit I've only postponed answering the question. I've discussed how a joke that doesn't work isn't tragedy. It might even be a camouflaged blessing. But the question remains: "What do you do when the jokes fail?"

Okay. Here are a few tips:

Forge boldly ahead: Don't let any disturbance disrupt your presentation more than momentarily. No turmoil should completely disrupt your talk. Recognize it, assess it, then proceed as well as you can—even when your bad joke is the "disturbance."

When I first began as an amateur public speaker, long before I became a writer, I hired a sound company to record my routine. I was going to have a hit record like Bob Newhart and Shelley Berman. The engineer placed microphones strategically throughout the audience to record the laughter. He had me miked properly. He did a great job. I didn't.

Everything I did bombed. It was awful, and it was painful. All I wanted to do was get the evening over with, slither off the stage, pay the nice man for his work, and go home for a good cry. First I had a lesson to learn.

The sound engineer chastised me. I thought, "I don't have enough trouble. I just stunk up the auditorium in front of my friends, now the guy in the headset is going to torment me."

I said, "I had a bad night. The jokes just weren't working. What was I supposed to do?"

He said, "You're supposed to work harder. Your first few jokes didn't work, so you quit."

He was right. I abandoned all energy and enthusiasm. I just recited the words. I destroyed any joke that had a chance to work. The audience was trying to make me a success, but I bailed out on them.

You have to keep going with increased passion. When things aren't going right, you need to challenge the listeners—confront them. You have to say in your own mind, "I'm going to give the rest of this performance everything I've got. Right now it's not looking too good, but when it's over, if it hasn't worked, it won't be because I surrendered."

John Wooden, the incredibly successful coach of UCLA's basketball team, claims that he never once mentioned winning to any of his players. He urged them only to do their best. His theory was that giving your best is all you can do. If you're good enough to win, you will. If not, you won't. That's out of your jurisdiction. But you can always give everything you've got.

That's good advice in doing humor, too. Give it a lot of excitement and zeal. If it doesn't work, then there's not much more you can do about it.

Acknowledge the failure: When a joke misfires, admit it. You don't have to humiliate yourself from the podium, but if a gag falls flat, don't be the only one in the hall who doesn't notice it.

Don't get carried away, either. If a piece of humor gets a moderate response, that's not a failure. Remember we advised that not every joke is a giant laugh-getter. Some are just chuckles. No, we're talking about the bombs. The ones that get no response beyond a stare. Those you own up to.

I've heard comics say after a non-joke, "Boy, and I thought that was going to be my biggie."

Bob Hope did a clinker on board ship off the coast of Beirut. He told the cue card guy to "roll that joke up in a big ball and fire it towards the enemy—if we can ever figure out who they are."

Sharing your frustration with the audience gains sympathy. It also invites them to have some fun along with you, and at your expense.

One reason for using humor is to gain the respect of your listeners. This reaffirms it. It convinces the audience that you know how your material is being received and that you're strong enough to deal with it if it's not going as well as you expected.

Prepare some "savers": Tim Conway used to get laughs at rehearsals of *The Carol Burnett Show.* Any time his scripted lines didn't get laughs from the staff and crew, he'd mutter audibly, "Saver, saver, saver."

A saver is a line that salvages an unfunny scripted line. Conway would stockpile them and spring them as adlibs during the taping. That's why Harvey Korman struggled for nine years to keep a straight face when working with Tim.

They're not a bad idea for your presentation, either. You won't need that many because you're not going to have that many humorous pieces misfire. Most of the time your humor is going to crackle. When it doesn't, though, a "saver" filed away in your memory can turn your flop into a fantastic funny.

Don't resort to savers promiscuously. They're not for humor that works moderately well; they're for gags that flop. If you use them too often, the audience is going to get the impression that your material isn't working. That could backfire on you.

Here are a few examples of savers. Each of these follows a joke that has not worked.

"My wife told me that story would never work. I can see you all side with her."

"I wasn't going to do that joke, then I changed my mind. I can see as I glance around the audience that my first instincts were correct."

"You'll have to forgive me; that's the first time I ever tried that story in public—and the last." (That might earn you applause.)

"That's my favorite joke and nobody ever laughs at it but me. I don't care; I'm going to keep telling it. I have to have some fun up here, too, you know."

"You won't hear that joke ever again—anywhere. I kind of wish you hadn't heard it tonight."

(If you want to kid somebody that the audience all know.)

"That's the last time I ever buy a joke from Mr. So-and-So."

8. Be aware of your audience and alter your routine: While you're doing all of the above, also notice what your audience likes and dislikes. Often there is a pattern that you can use to your advantage.

They may like the short jokes, but not sit still for the longer stories. They may not enjoy being kidded about themselves, but laugh at the material about the competition.

Each audience will be different, but you may learn from listening to them when some of your pieces don't get the response you expect.

You've probably heard a nightclub comedian tell a slightly naughty gag (or a downright dirty one), and after the laugh say something like, "Oh, it's that kind of a group, huh?" That comic is probably not kidding. He or she might have tried that gag out just to test the waters. It will determine what the rest of the entertainment will be like.

If the only pattern you notice is that this crowd doesn't enjoy any of your humor, then—"If in doubt, cut it." Cut your comedy and just offer your message.

What do I do when the jokes don't work? Well, if that ever happens to me, I'll get back to you. Yes, that's my standard reply and it usually gets a laugh. Why? Because everyone knows that sometime, somewhere, a joke is going to fall flat. It happens to everyone. It happens to me; it happens to Bob Hope; it'll happen to you. It's no big deal.

The big deal is to continue to use humor well and wisely, understanding that once in a while it won't work. Don't fear that. Don't be afraid of your audience. They won't attack when the gags fall short. Go out there and have a little fun with them. If a joke or two doesn't work, have fun with that. The audience is friendly. Be friendly back. Enough of your humor will work. Trust me.

CHAPTER EIGHTEEN

How Do I Avoid Offending Anyone?

Consider this harmless little ditty that you may have heard in your early elementary school days:

> Roses are red,
>   Violets are blue,
> You look like a monkey
>   And you smell like one too.

I called that harmless, but is it? If you were to use that from the platform or in some publication, you might get notes from any of the following:

An irate florist might chide you for using roses as a weapon of insult. Traditionally, the rose has been a symbol of love and romance. How dare you demean this lovely bud by using it to introduce such a blatantly offensive message?

An infuriated botanist may tell you that violets are not blue. They are the most captivating shades of violet, hence the name. To call them blue is to diminish their allure.

A zoologist might be incensed by your disparaging comments about one of God's most enchanting creatures—the monkey. Don't you realize that their intellect is very close to man? Don't you appreciate the good they've done for humanity, say—in the space program—to name just one? Don't you understand that an animal's odor is part of his survival mechanism, that it serves a purpose in the wild? Those innocent little animals are as clean, if not cleaner, than you are.

In doing humor, should you worry about those pen-pals: the florist, the botanist, and the zoologist? I don't think so. There are those people who are inordinately defensive about anything that concerns them. They have no sense of humor about themselves. Those folks have a problem that is beyond the scope of this book. If we limited our humor because of them, there would be no laughter left in the world.

This doesn't allow us humorists carte blanche to attack anyone with immunity. Often the complaints against us are valid. For instance, not all used car salesmen are thieves; not all mothers-in-law are battle-axes. We should avoid unfounded generalizations, gratuitous accusations.

(In fact, I should apologize to the florists, botanists, and zoologists of the world. I didn't mean to discredit them.)

As a humorist, you have to separate honest protesters from humorless cranks.

There is one person you need to be concerned about in this example, though. That's the guy or gal you're saying it to. You've just told someone that he or she smells like a monkey. Despite what the zoologist contends, that's generally presumed to be an insult.

Now there's "malice aforethought." You've aimed a jest directly at a specific person. You maligned that person's odor. You're guilty.

Does that mean that you can't do humor like this? No, it means that you need to be aware of your audience and aware of the consequences of your comedy.

Humor, as we've seen, can be a powerful communication tool However, like most power it must be handled carefully. It can misfire, backfire, or simply be abused.

Humor can hurt others intentionally. It can be used not as a tool, but as a weapon. I don't advocate that. To me, humor is a valuable asset, and I hate to see it misused.

However, it might be used effectively as a device that doesn't injure, but stings. I remember once when our community had a problem with its roads. Streets were in dangerous disrepair. Community groups went through channels, went around channels, and invented some new channels, but the authorities paid no attention. The streets went unrepaired. Then a local columnist did a satire on our streets in the community paper. It was so scathingly funny that the city fathers finally fixed the potholes. They did it to get that "comedian" off their backs.

That kind of humor might have been a little painful for some, but it was necessary. It was like the prick of a vaccination. Its long term benefits outweighed its short term unpleasantness.

Humor can also hurt others unintentionally. That's what we all want to avoid. Our humor is used to enhance communication, not to wound innocent parties. And, any humor that wounds another, even unintentionally, hurts our presentation. It creates an unnecessary tension that distracts from our message.

Have you ever been a houseguest where your hosts were having a spat? Even if no angry words are exchanged, the silent animosity is upsetting. If the argument is verbal, it's worse. You don't feel comfortable in that situation. You either want them to settle the dispute or you want to leave. That's the way your audience feels when your humor is offensive, even unintentionally.

Your first safeguard against injurious comedy is your attitude. What's in your mind when you create or deliver it? Is it revenge? Spite? Ego? "I'll show them?" All of these are dangerous. Your humor can develop a cutting edge that could put off your listeners.

If your attitude is a spirit of fun, your humor is more secure. It shouldn't hurt. Take, for example, these lines complaining about our income tax system:

> "The new simplified tax forms have only three questions: How much did you make? How much do you have left? How soon can you send it in?"

> "Here's a way the government can really simplify income tax returns. Just print our money with a return address on it."

> "They say you can't get blood from a stone—unless you work for the IRS."

Are these vicious, scathing lines condemning an unfair tariff? I doubt it. They're good-natured, humorous jabs at a necessary evil. As Will Rogers, the beloved American humorist—who did as many jokes about income tax as anyone—said, "America is a great country, but you can't live in it for nothing."

Consider, too, our opening four-line poem, "You look like a monkey, and you smell like one too." Is that an offensive line or some friendly kidding? You can't tell because you don't have enough information. You have to know what was behind it. Was it meant to hurt or was it meant to tease?

The proper attitude in using humor is your first safeguard, but it's not a guarantee. Humor, even when delivered in fun, can sometimes offend. I don't mean the kind of offense that our thin-skinned florist, botanist, and zoologist felt. I mean a real hurt that you regret.

Even Will Rogers, who warned us not to have any malice in our humor, sometimes offended people. In 1926, at a banquet of the Old Trail Drivers Association in San Antonio, Rogers was honored by Mrs. R.R. Russell of the Ladies Auxiliary. She pinned an honorary membership badge on the comedian and sat next to him through the banquet. When Rogers spoke he said, "You Old Trail Drivers . . . did all right. You'd start out down here with nothing, and after stealing our cattle in the Indian Nation, you'd wind up in Abilene with 2,000 head or more."

Mrs. Russell stood up and shouted, "My husband was no cattle thief. Don't insinuate that he was."

Newspaper photos of the event show that Mrs. Russell was not at all pleased with Rogers' after dinner oratory. I don't blame her. I'm a Will Rogers fan, and even though he meant no harm—there was no malice in his heart—this seemed like the wrong gag to use at this banquet.

There are a few ways that humor can be hurtful.

Misinterpretation

As a creative exercise in some of my humor seminars, I have people work with words. We take a basic, simple word—"A common ordinary word, something you might find around the house," as Groucho Marx used to say on *You Bet Your Life*—then we try to find several other meanings for that word.

To show you what I mean, let's use the word "house" as an example. We all feel we know the meaning of that word. We can picture it clearly in our minds. Are you picturing, though, the same thing that I'm picturing when I use the word house? We don't know. We don't have enough information.

With very little effort, I'll bet you can find about seven valid, recognized, everyday uses for the word "house." Try it. Close the book for a few minutes and see how many different uses of the word "house" you can come up with. When you're done, come back and read the ones listed here:

1) a dwelling

2) a gambling casino, as in "house rules," or "the house takes a percentage of the bet."

3) a branch of our government

4) a bordello, as in "a house is not a home."

5) attendance at a theatre, as in "count the house."

6) a family or dynasty, as in the "house of David"

7) to contain, as in "the museum will house the original autobiography of Benjamin Franklin."

There are probably others. You can do this exercise with many common words, including some that might surprise you. The word "butterfly," for example, might have several different meanings. It's the pretty little critter that floats around flowers; it's also what they do to a filet mignon when you ask for it well done; it's also the queasy feeling you get in the pit of your stomach when you're nervous. You could probably uncover a few more.

Why bring that up here, when we're discussing humor that might be offensive? Because it's a potential area of misunderstanding. If you're not careful with your words, listeners can misinterpret them.

I once wrote a parody of Cinderella for a nightclub act. Several notable people of the day were cast as characters in that fairytale. One very well-known politician was the "Fairy Godfather." He was the good guy in the parody. He was a well-liked public figure and I thought making him the hero would be a smart idea.

It wasn't. People got angry at this piece of material because of the negative implications involved in the role. Can you guess why?

Right. The use of the word "Fairy" led many people to think that we were comedically implying that this official was homosexual. That was never intended and nothing else in the parody could have led anyone in the audience to assume that. It was strictly a misreading of one word—yet it was a common word. The woman in the original was called the "Fairy Godmother," so it seemed natural that a man in the parody would be named "Fairy Godfather."

"Godfather" was the other troublesome word. Since 1972 and the award-winning film, "Godfather" connotes a mob leader. Listeners felt that we were implying gang connections by calling this politician a "Godfather," even though nothing else in the script insinuated that.

We had to drop the routine, an otherwise funny one, from the nightclub act. It angered, rather than entertained.

There's another interesting aspect of communication. It's a mind-to-mind intercourse. It sounds simple. You say something and people hear it. But, it's more complicated. In fact, the message goes through at least four steps.

First, it must exist in your mind, the mind of the speaker. You have to know what you're going to say.

Second, you translate your thought to words; and that translation is not always accurate. You may not say what you mean. Words are not ideas; they're just descriptions of ideas. You may not choose or be able to find the words that say exactly what you're thinking. We haven't even gotten past the speaker yet and already we have several areas for misunderstanding.

Third, people have to hear your words. They don't always hear what you say. We always kid about a language we used to use in my hometown of South Philadelphia—it was a language that was peculiar to that part of town. For instance, what is meant by the phrase, "Jeet jet?" It means, "Have you had your dinner?". So when one of my buddies says, "Jeet jet?" that's exactly what people hear, but that's not what he meant. He meant, "Did you eat yet?". It's another chance for error.

Fourth, whatever the people hear—whether it's what we said, or not; whether it's what we meant to say, or not—now must be interpreted in their minds. The words they hear become ideas, and we've already noted that words can only approximate ideas.

So you have to think something and then say what you think you thought—although it might not be the thought you think you thought. You have to say what you're thinking, but you might only be saying what you're saying—and not what you think you're saying— which is what you thought. Someone has to hear what you think you're saying, but it could be what they think you said and not what you thought you said. To them, then, what you think you said is not what they think you said. They think about what you thought you said and think they know what you thought, but they only think they know your thoughts. Get it?

Now if that explanation doesn't prove that the process is ripe for misunderstanding, then you've misunderstood my whole point.

Before being reelected to his second term in office, Ronald Reagan addressed a group of young people at a drug rehabilitation center.

"When you get along to where I am," the 72-year-old President said, "you find out that taking care of that machinery (your body) sure pays off when . . . you can still tie your shoes and pull on your own socks without sitting down—and do a lot of things that are much more enjoyable than that." The President smiled.

The young audience, though, laughed. Why? They thought it was a reference to sex. Reagan later explained that he was talking about riding horses, chopping wood, swimming, and diving.

Regardless of what he meant, the audience heard "sex."

This just proves that you must consider your words carefully in communicating. Since humor often skirts the boundaries of respectability, it's even more important that you convey your meaning exactly.

Review the humor you use. Double check for double entendres. I don't mean the blue material type of double entendre—I mean innocent words that could have a second or third meaning.

I recently spoke to a group of pharmacists. I had to, at their request, be sure that I didn't use the word "drugs." These people are pharmacists and they dispense medicine. "Drugs" in today's culture has a new meaning that they rightfully disassociate themselves from.

In speaking to politicians, the word "fix" may be off limits. You and I "fix" a flat tire; politicians "adjust" a flat tire.

Also, look for hidden meanings in your humor. Can it be misinterpreted? Are you really saying what you mean? Or are you going to be like the man who said, "I'm an atheist. I swear to God I am;" or the radio broadcaster who said, " . . . this movie stars Burt Reynolds and Dolly Parton. Boy, what a pair!"

Beware of related issues

Suppose you're the banquet speaker and you want to kid the president of the organization, so you pick some standard, universal topic that applies to almost everyone. You decide to kid him about his marriage.

> "During dinner Charlie and I were talking about marriage. He told me he never knew what true happiness was until he got married—then it was too late."

> "Charlie told me that he and his wife have a perfect 50-50 arrangement. Every time he makes 50, she spends 50."

> "Charlie's wife is with him on this trip. She likes to make the trips with him. Well, wouldn't you? It's easier than kissing him goodbye."

Those feel like fairly harmless gags and you certainly want to deliver them in a spirit of fun. Some kid him, some kid her, so you avoid taking sides. These jokes might get a laugh, but not if everyone in the association knows that Charlie and Mrs. Charlie are in the process of filing for divorce.

Related circumstances can change the nature of your humor.

I manufactured that example. Of course, if you were going to kid with such personal material, you should have checked to make sure it's all right. But, some of the other examples I've seen and heard are too unpleasant to repeat!

I once saw a young comic get booed off the stage in a comedy club when he did a routine about children. A horrible kidnapping had been in that town's newspapers for the past week. His material, which flirted with bad taste to begin with, became grotesque.

It's impossible to think up all the situations that might arise, because there are so many variables, but you should be aware that even the most innocent material can be affected by situations that you may know nothing about.

If you can't know about these things, how can you protect against them? First, be aware of possible dangers. If you're going to tease a man about his marriage, find out about that marriage first. Check with people who know him well.

Second, be aware of potential danger in your own material. Would some of it border on the edge of propriety under normal conditions? If it does, it won't take much to push it over that edge. Question the use of that material. Even if you decide it is acceptable, check with someone who knows the group to make sure you won't offend this particular audience.

Some areas that might be trouble: stories about drinking, traffic accidents, death, physical disabilities. You get the idea. Double check any humor that might be described as "black comedy."

Even perfectly innocent jokes can backfire. I check material in one of two ways when I speak to associations. I very quickly review my presentation with my contact, the program chairman, the association president, or whoever. Not so they can evaluate the effectiveness of it, but so they can warn me of anything that's potentially offensive. Second, at a cocktail party or hospitality suite before my talk, I tell a few of the anecdotes to individuals or small groups. The reaction they get at that level can warn me what to use and what to cut from the presentation.

If your material is tasteful and considerate to begin with, an adverse audience reaction is rare and usually not disastrous. Nevertheless, once aware of the potential dangers, you can take reasonable precautions.

Insult humor

This has to be offensive, right? After all, it is insult humor. Webster defines "insult" as "gross abuse offered to another either by words or actions; any act or speech meant to hurt the feelings or self-respect of another." That sounds pretty offensive, doesn't it?

Suppose you see two men meeting at an annual convention. They know each other, but they haven't met in a year. They shake hands politely and exchange greetings:

"How are you?"
"Fine. And yourself?"
"Not bad. Did you just get in?"
"Yes. I haven't even checked in yet."
"Well, I'll see you around."
"Yes, I'll be at the party tonight."

And they part.

Now picture two other men who meet at the same convention. They haven't seen each other all year, either.

"Boy, they let anyone into this hotel, don't they?"

"Hey, how are you? You know, you get uglier every time I see you."

"Look who's talking. I love that suit you got. I understand that style is coming back."

"You going to be at the party tonight?"

"Not if you're going to be there, I'm not."

"Let's have a drink later. You're buying."

"I'm sure I am. You haven't picked up a tab since 1976."

And they part.

Don't you agree that the first two guys were probably acquaintances, and the second two were most likely close buddies? Insult humor is an acceptable form of social behavior today. Especially so since the Friars and Dean Martin's television show popularized "the roast."

Insult jokes are acceptable, but they're delicate. I've found them powerful and useful. But they must be handled with care.

Follow these rules:

1. Kid people about what they kid themselves about: When people kid themselves, they're usually giving notice that they're not sensitive about that topic. Sometimes, granted, it is their way of masking how they really feel—only they know that for sure. But it's never safe to assume that you can kid people about anything. Some bald people laugh at their baldness; others won't admit they're bald and don't want you bringing it up. Some companies readily admit that Project X from last year was an unqualified flop; other companies don't want their dirty linen aired at the annual awards banquet.

However, if you attend a few seminars and everyone is joking about Project X, you can assume that one or two tasteful lines at the banquet won't offend anyone.

2. Kid about things that don't matter: Bob Hope has kidded every President who ever was in office. Most of the barbs, though, are inoffensive. Why? Because when you analyze them, they're not really about the issues. They're simply kidding a man in a very visible office about something entirely apart from his job.

For example, Hope kids Gerald Ford constantly about his golf:

"You never have to count strokes when you play with Jerry Ford. You just look back along the fairway and count the wounded."

"You can always spot Jerry Ford on the golf course. His cart is the one with the red cross painted on top."

"There are over 150 golf courses in the Palm Springs area, and Jerry Ford is never sure which one he's going to play until his second shot."

None of those passes judgment on Ford's tenure as President. They don't dispute any of his policies. They simply kid his golf game. No politician lives or dies on his golf handicap.

A relatively safe topic to select for insult humor is one that's far away from a nerve, one that avoids any real controversy.

3. Kid about things that are so bizarre that no one can take them seriously: If everyone knows you're kidding, the malice disappears from the insult. Everyone—at least every-reasonable-one—should know you're kidding if what you're saying can't possibly be true.

I once did a monologue at a party for my Mom. I kidded her about how she kept my brothers and me so neat and clean when we were young:

"Mom used to keep my brothers and me so clean that we always thought we were for sale."

"Mom put starch in everything. I sneezed once and cut my nose on a handkerchief."

"Everything we owned had starch in it. My brother fell out of bed one night and broke his pajamas."

No one could think ill of Mom from those gags because no one could believe any of them.

Those rules will help keep your insult humor from being insulting. Be careful, though. Just following them doesn't guarantee that any humor you do will be inoffensive. Your attitude is important, too. If there's malice in your heart, there can be malice in your jokes, even if they adhere to these guidelines. Keep your humor humorous. Insult in a spirit of fun and you'll be safe.

Check out insult material carefully. Get a second opinion from someone who knows. And follow this book's standard edict: "If in doubt, cut it."

CHAPTER NINETEEN

Pitfalls That Take the Fun Out of Humor

I once spoke at a company function and did a whole routine about a duplicating machine in our department. This wasn't a simple little reproducing machine that you see in today's modern offices. This was an ammonia blueprinting machine that reproduced drawings up to six-feet-wide and practically unlimited length. It was a large, expensive contraption that never worked properly.

That's what my jokes were about. I kidded about this being a valuable machine to have in a drafting office; it ate harmful blueprints. I made some management-oriented crack about it working less than someone whose brother-in-law was the shop steward. Gags like that.

I thought they were funny. One gentleman didn't. He was the supervisor of the department that operated and maintained the machine. He was under some pressure from his manager, who surely was under pressure from his vice-president, to get the machine functioning consistently and efficiently. He was hurt and embarrassed by my routine and left the banquet.

The jokes were funny; the evening wasn't fun for me or for him.

The purpose of the humor we've discussed in this book is to enhance your message. It's to get people to listen and remember what you say. It is easier to do that when you amuse, entertain, and refresh your audience.

Humor is not the only device that accomplishes this. In your business communication you may resort to shock value at times. Perhaps threats work on occasion. Offering rewards can get people to listen and act. All of these are valid devices along with many other dramatic ones. They're all beyond the scope of this volume, though. We're discussing humor as a communications tool. It isn't always "belly laugh" comedy. It can produce a chuckle, a smile, a grin, or even just a raised eyebrow and a nod of recognition. But it should be fun.

Anything that interferes with that fun interferes with this message.

There are a few booby traps to be aware of:

1. Humor that's too aggressive: Generally, this is humor that's not designed to entertain or amuse; it's meant to punish. It's not there to enhance a presentation; it's there to gain an unfair advantage in a personal battle.

The example that I used to begin this chapter was an honest misjudgment on my part. I was speaking at a company function to company executives, and I joked about something that mattered. But common sense should have warned me that someone would get hurt.

Suppose, though, that my department had been feuding with this supervisor's department over that duplicating machine. Let's say that my work was being delayed because he refused to take the time or spend the money to fix the machine. Then my jokes would have a new meaning. They would have shown upper management that this gentleman's department was a liability. The laughs from the audience would have indicated that the whole facility knew how ridiculous this outdated piece of machinery was.

It would have worked, too; but it wouldn't have been humor—at least not the productive type of humor we're talking about in this book.

Aggressive humor is like the kids in the schoolyard who quarrel with childish "Oh yeah? Well, your mother wears army boots," type of invectives. The one with the most supporters gets the most derisive laughs, and wins.

Some use this aggressive humor (or aggression disguised as humor) to fight personal battles. They convert the microphone and the podium to offensive assault weapons.

Aggressive humor is almost always offensive—in both meanings of the word. It antagonizes and it attacks.

I heard a business speaker once who was angry because he had gotten a citation while driving to the meetingplace. He wove his revenge into his presentation. He exhorted his listeners to set goals and establish priorities. "Don't be like the local police force. Don't be handing out traffic tickets while there are rapists and drug dealers roaming the streets."

He expected a laugh and a roar of "Hear, hear!" from the crowd. He got disapproval. It wasn't appropriate for him as a luncheon speaker to be fighting his private wars. Besides, how could this audience side with him when they didn't know any of the facts? If he was driving through their neighborhood at 80 miles an hour, he deserved the ticket. His sarcastic remarks aimed at their police were offensive.

It annoyed the audience because they realized they were being used to fight a personal battle—a battle that shouldn't involve them. They resented being forced to stand in the schoolyard while the speaker shouted names at his foe.

It may be all right to become offensive if you're the spokesman for your listeners in a common cause. In the preceding chapter we learned how a columnist attacked with humor and won a battle with the city leaders over potholes in the street. Everybody in the neighborhood wanted those holes fixed. This writer was verbalizing a common complaint. It was a community fight, not a personal vendetta.

As a speaker, you have an obligation to your listeners. They resent it when you use their time to attack windmills that only you see.

2. Humor that divides your audience: One of the sweetest sounds in the world (for humorists, anyway) is an explosion of laughter from an audience. The entire crowd laughs on cue. A humorist wants to entertain the entire audience; a speaker wants to enlighten the entire audience. So avoid anything that will divide your listeners.

Don't let your humor begin a mini-civil war, dividing brother against brother. Don't use anecdotes that set Democrats against Republicans, management against labor, men against women.

At a company retirement banquet I heard an upper management speaker praise the guest of honor for his loyalty during a recent strike. He said, "Not too long ago you could throw a rolled-up paper across the office and the only persons you would hit would be exempt employees and Good Old Charlie."

Awkward silence followed. The remark wasn't fair to either Good Old Charlie or the audience. It wasn't really meant to praise Charlie. There were better ways to do that. It was there to get a little dig in at the union. And it did.

It also resurrected all the animosity of the recent strike. It recalled the bitterness between the strikers and the executives. It even reminded everyone that Good Old Charlie was a "scab" in the minds of many of his fellow workers.

Divisive humor doesn't serve the speaker, either. It creates a tension that distracts an audience. You want people to pay attention to your remarks, hear them, and remember them. Separate your listeners into two or more factions and rather than accepting your words, their minds will be busy formulating their rebuttal.

Surely, you've relived an unpleasant encounter in your own mind. Someone annoyed you with an obnoxious remark, then you spent a good portion of your day fantasizing. "I should have said this or that." "Boy, if he had only done this, I would have done that." You're distracted. Your mind can't see the present for reconstructing the past. That's what happens to an audience when you divide. They don't listen to your words because they're too busy speaking their own inside their heads.

Divisive comedy also irritates a portion of your audience. They like you less than when you started. Rather than hearing your message and analyzing it, they begin looking for flaws in your argument. They search for reasons to disbelieve what you say. No speaker wants that.

But don't political humorists like Bob Hope and Johnny Carson divide the audience? When they do a joke about a Democratic president, don't they lose the Republicans? Not necessarily, because they're not really taking sides. They joke about authority, about the office of President. If a Republican gets elected, they'll kid him while he's in office. If a Democrat wins the election, he'll be kidded just the same.

That's a good example, though, of how humor and the attitude behind it can either be fun or divisive. Most of us forgive Hope and Carson for their comments about a liberal politician. But if a Bill Buckley made the same comment about a liberal, it would be offensive.

3. Humor that destroys your dignity: You've seen this shtick dozens of times: a comic takes a gulp of water, turns to speak to the audience, and the water dribbles out of his mouth, down his chin, and onto his shirt and tie. It gets a laugh.

The Three Stooges poked eyes, pulled hair, and pounded each other on top of the head.

Gallagher, a bright comedian, ends his act by smashing food with a sledge hammer. The big finale is a watermelon squashing. Fans bring clear plastic sheets so they can sit in the front rows without getting splashed.

Very few CEO's use these gimmicks.

Any humor you use in a business speech that lessens your dignity might be costly. The fun content of your presentation is supposed to help the audience receive it. If instead, they lose respect for the speaker, the message will be hurt. People won't trust or respect you and your credibility will be damaged.

Picture yourself in an emergency with a group of others. Who would you select as your leader? A person of quiet wit or the guy who tries to impress young ladies by removing his dentures and swallowing his nose with his lower lip?

Physical, slapstick comedy is not the only way you can diminish your dignity. Off-color jokes can do it; sick jokes can do it; almost anything in bad taste can do it. Say and do only those things that are consistent with your stature.

Not all physical comedy is undesirable for the business speaker. I once saw an awards presenter effectively use an ancient piece of comedy business. He presented a rose to a young woman. When she took the step to accept, the presenter kept the rose, and she held only the stem. It got a big laugh. He explained, "This is just like our travel expenses. The accounting department gives us most of it, but what they hold back is critical." He then presented the rose to the woman. It was physical humor, but pleasant and tasteful.

Tastefulness is the key. See and hear yourself doing your humor as a person in the audience might see and hear you. Then judge for yourself: when you watch and listen, are you proud of it? Do you maintain your dignity? If you don't, or you're not sure, don't do it.

People don't enjoy buffoonery, except when professional clowns and comics do it. It's demeaning. It insults their intelligence for a speaker to think they would enjoy this type of comedy.

The comment I heard most often about the Academy Awards telecast of 1988 focuses on this issue. Emcee Chevy Chase introduced Paul Newman as one of the presenters. When Newman reached the lectern, Chase chatted with him for a moment or two. They discussed the dignity of this affair and how prestigious an evening it was. When

Chevy Chase turned the lectern over to Paul Newman, he took about five steps and his pants fell down.

Paul Newman looked at him standing there in his shorts and said, "I suppose there's something to be said for comedy."

People I spoke to, remarked, "How could he do that to Paul Newman?" Newman added some class to the evening, and this shtick detracted from it.

When you step on the podium, you should add class to the proceedings. That's an important part of the image you need to convey to your listeners. That's prerequisite to their respecting you and listening to your remarks. Anything that detracts from your dignity lessens the impact of your speech.

4. Humor that embarrasses your audience (or any member of your audience): I once attended a convention where a featured speaker was an image coordinator. He taught business men and women how to dress properly and fashionably for the office, for travel, and so on. He was scheduled to speak at various times during the convention, and most people were planning to attend his sessions. Everyone wants to dress impressively and correctly.

I was there for his first speech, and it was quite crowded. He brought about a dozen men and women onstage and asked the audience to look at them for awhile and silently analyze how they were dressed. Were they dressed attractively? Did they inspire confidence? Would they make a good impression on clients?

After the audience evaluated them, he did. He took each person individually and critiqued his or her outfit.

He pointed out that one man was wearing a polyester sports jacket. He said, "The best thing about this jacket is that it will never burn. The worst thing about this jacket is that it will never burn." He advised that the jacket should be burned and then pointed out everything that was wrong with the jacket. It was cheap; it was outdated; it was tacky; it was unfashionable. He even added as a final insult, "A Nehru jacket might be preferable."

He wanted to be funny. Was he? Well, there were scattered laughs throughout the audience, nervous laughs. But he wasn't funny to the man in the polyester jacket. He wasn't funny to the friends of the man in the polyester jacket. He wasn't funny to most of the audience who sympathized with the man in the polyester jacket.

He embarrassed the volunteer onstage and a good percentage of the listeners. It got worse.

He told one woman her dress was fashionable and perfect for travel, "if you're accompanying your husband across the plains in a covered wagon."

The next time he spoke, few people were in the audience. Curiosity prompted most of those who did attend. They wanted to see if this man was as horrendous as everyone said he was.

He frightened listeners away for two reasons: they were afraid of being singled out for ridicule, and they didn't want to see others embarrassed.

This man's message was good. He offered invaluable tips about fashion, colors, materials, how to shop for clothing, prices to pay, and plenty of other useful information. After that first session, however, no one wanted to hear it. Wait, let me change that: They still wanted to hear it; but they didn't want to hear it from him.

Those who did hear it, rejected it. The man quickly became so unlikable onstage that no one would listen to what he had to say. Even though he was right, they refused to accept it.

We could come to his defense. We could say that those who stepped onstage, volunteering for a critique, were inviting negative comments. Of course, they were. They probably expected errors in their ensemble and wanted him to point this out. There is a way to offer constructive criticism, though, without embarrassing and alienating your audience. It can be done safely with humor.

I have seen another speaker, a very successful business lecturer, who invites members of her audience onstage to become contestants in a male beauty pageant. She is a former Miss America contestant, and she wants the men in her audience to feel what that is like.

Her purpose is not to embarrass these men, but to have fun with them. She teases them, tricks them into making dumb mistakes, asks them foolish questions, and then points out the foolishness of their answers. The men enjoy themselves and so does the audience.

What's the difference? First, she checks with her potential "beauty contestants." She warns them about the gimmick. She doesn't rehearse them or tell them specifically what she will say or do—the whole thing is spontaneous—but she does tell them that she will tease and kid them. She seeks outgoing men. Those who would rather not participate can just say so.

Second, her kidding is harmless. Some of it is insulting, but as we saw in an earlier chapter, you can insult without offending.

Third, her humor is generalized, not specific. The person in her presentation is not singled out for a vicious attack. He's the representative of the audience. The audience senses that whatever she is saying to him, she could just as well be saying to them. Whatever she tricks him into, she could have tricked the audience into, also. When they laugh at him, they laugh at themselves. "There but for the grace of God, go I," they might say.

Fourth, her attitude is important. The show is fun. It has a message, but the humor content is fun. Her attitude says to her volunteers, "We're going to have a good time up here. I like you, and when we're done, I'm sure you'll like me." The audience senses that and none of her joking embarrasses anyone.

Unlike our earlier example, this speaker attracts more and bigger audiences. When people hear how much fun her show is, they want to attend and participate.

Beware of embarrassing your audience. It's not only onstage participation that can do it. Stories, anecdotes, and comments can humiliate, too. If you ridicule a person at the head table without good cause, you can lose your audience. Blue material can embarrass an audience. They may laugh the nervous laugh, but many of them won't want to see you again.

5. Humor that hurts: We've already discussed insult humor and how to use it without offending. However, there are other ways of hurting people with comedy and not all of them are foreseeable. For instance, I once did a show with a comic who liked to use aggressive humor. When he went into the audience for some questions-and-answers, he said to a young man in a striped tee shirt, "Oh, look, here's a kid who's dressed like a pirate."

The "pirate" was a guest of one of our writers, who told us later that the young man was very upset by the remark. He didn't understand why this comedian was calling him a pirate.

How do you protect against that? Well, sometimes you don't—you can't. All you can do is review the humor content of your speech and be aware of your audience. If you know something will hurt, take it out. If you are not sure, replace it anyway.

CHAPTER TWENTY

Humor in the Workplace

A writing friend of mine had a unique criteria for accepting or rejecting freelance assignments. He'd caution himself, "If it ain't fun, don't do it." It was an effective, if ungrammatical, philosophy for him, but for most of us it's hardly practical.

In the 40-hour-a-week/50-week-a-year world, we don't have that kind of control over which assignments we land, or what sort of headaches come with each assignment. However, we can amend that writer's advice: "If it ain't fun, make it fun."

We spend about a third of our lives in the workplace. With a little effort, we can make it as pleasant as the other two-thirds of our life. We can use our humor and our sense of humor just as effectively to benefit ourselves as we can in our communications to benefit our audience.

Can humor change the facts? Can it transform a negative to a positive? No. But nothing is totally negative or totally positive. And, as the song says, it helps to "accentuate the positive and eliminate the negative."

How can we use humor every day in the workplace?

First, we can be aware of its power. Humor is an attitude, an outlook; a thinking process. We can control our thinking. But we have to remember to do it, and often we have to make a conscious effort to do it.

Most success philosophies stress that our thoughts control our behavior. *Think and Grow Rich* was Napoleon Hill's best-selling title. *The Magic of Believing* was Claude Bristol's. Norman Vincent Peale wrote *The Power of Positive Thinking*. They all say we are what we think. Think happy and we become happier.

Bob Hope told me a story that illustrates this. He was travelling with his radio troupe during World War II. They were broadcasting from various battle zones, entertaining the troops. While they were flying from one base to another on a military plane, officers advised them to put on their life jackets.

The plane was in trouble and the crew thought they might have to make a forced landing on water. Hope said that there was fear and anxiety on everyone's face—except for Jerry Colonna's. When Hope looked at him, Colonna just shrugged his shoulders and made a face that said, "I might as well put the jacket on. There's not much else I can do about it."

Hope told me that Colonna's reaction was so unexpected, and the face he made so hilarious that, despite the crisis, everyone laughed. The rubber-faced comedian wanted to lighten the situation and he did.

"It just snapped us all out of it," Hope said. The emergency still existed, but the morale improved because of Colonna's attitude.

The aircraft landed safely, but this incident must have made a deep impression on Hope. He told me the story over 40 years after it happened.

That story points out another benefit of a sense of humor—it's catching. Colonna's attitude affected the others.

It's the opposite of a vicious circle. Humor creates a pleasant atmosphere, which makes everyone else more pleasant, which makes it easier for us to be pleasant.

Second, we can keep focused on the present. Most worry goes on when we fictionalize or fantasize about imaginary problems, or magnify real problems. In stress most of us aggravate the trouble by projecting the worst possible scenario. We create or manufacture difficulties in our minds.

In the example above, there was a threat of a crash landing, but there wasn't a crash.

Humor is truth—it's reality. It enables us to see and react to what is happening, not what might happen or what could happen.

Life is much easier if we deal with the challenge that's confronting us, not with the one we create.

When I was scheduled for heart surgery a few years ago, I was frightened. The doctor told me that I was an excellent candidate for the surgery and that he expected no problems. But I expected problems. I worried about every unpleasant contingency, regardless of how unlikely.

Phyllis Diller called to cheer me up. I was determined to be uncheerable. She told me of many friends who had the same surgery and were revitalized. She told me that I'd be up and around in no time at all and feeling better than ever.

I said, "Phyllis, I know what you're saying, but I'm still scared." Phyllis, who kids herself about her many cosmetic surgeries, said, "Gene, just look on it as a chest lift."

I like the story of the cowboy in the old west who knew how to view things with a sense of reality and a sense of humor.

He was enjoying some drinks and a few hands of poker with some friends in the town saloon when a fierce desperado barged in. The villain drew his guns and shouted, "I want every yellow-bellied, snake-livered, slime-crawling, chicken-hearted, son of a sidewinder to clear out of here, or I'm gonna start shooting."

Chairs scraped on the floor, tables overturned, and patrons scrambled for the exits. The only one who remained was our hero.

The outlaw walked over to him, shoved his gun under his nose and repeated, "I said I wanted every yellow-bellied, snake-livered, slime-crawling, chicken-hearted, son of a sidewinder to clear out of here."

The cowboy said, "I heard you. There sure were a lot of them, weren't there?"

ABOUT THE AUTHOR

Gene Perret was born in Philadelphia, Pennsylvania, and worked for 13 years in the Electrical Drafting and Engineering Departments of General Electric's Switchgear Plant there.

He began his comedy writing and speaking career by emceeing company banquets and parties. His hobby became a full-time profession in 1969 when he left GE to write for Bob Hope, Phyllis Diller, Carol Burnett, Bill Cosby, Tim Conway, and many other stars and shows.

Gene has travelled extensively with Bob Hope including Command Performance shows for the 25th anniversary of the coronation of Queen Elizabeth II, and for King Gustav of Sweden. Gene also was the only writer to journey to the war zones of Beirut, Lebanon, and the Persian Gulf with Bob Hope's USO Christmas tours.

Today Perret writes for Bob Hope's personal appearances and television specials, and performs his own brand of after-dinner humor for many associations and corporations all across the country.

Gene and Joanne live in San Marino, CA. Their four children, Joe, Terry, Carole, and Linda are grown and on their own, so they concentrate on spoiling their two grandsons, Michael and Brett.

Index

Abbott, Bud, 180
Accidentals, 151–152
Adapting material, 88–89, 121–126, 149–157; exercises, 165–166, 168
All in the Family, 103
Allen, Woody, 65, 73, 134–135, 181
Anka, Paul, 100
Apocryphal stories, 113
Applying material to your message, 122–126, 165–167
Attention, audience, 21–23
Audience: attention, 21–23; attitude, 75–76, 182; laughter, 179–180; relation to, 148–149, 190–192, 196; testing, 49
Autry, Gene, 108

Baker, Jim and Tammy, 140–141
Ball, Lucille, 74
Barr, Roseanne, 74, 77
Beirut, Lebanon, 19, 194
Bennett, Alan, 163
Benny, Jack, 67, 78, 120, 127
Berle, Milton, 40, 45
Berman, Shelley, 189–190
Berra, Yogi, 118
Billings, Josh, 162
Black comedy, 204
Bob Hope Show, 19
Bombs, 185–196
Booby traps in humor, 210–216
Borge, Victor, 45
Braden, Vic, 86
Brenner, David, 38–39, 114
Bristol, Claude, 217
Buckley, William, 212
Burnett, Carol, 63, 148, 155, 183; see *Carol Burnett Show*
Burns, George, 64, 65, 74, 118, 154–155, 189
"Button," 108
Buttram, Pat, 108

Captions, 140, 160, 167, 168
Carol Burnett Show, 43, 45, 108, 148, 194
Carson, Johnny, 63, 67, 68, 74, 99, 136,

137, 140, 148, 186–187, 192–193, 212
Cartoon humor, 91
Cartoons: captions for, 167; personalized, 160
Cavett, Dick, 73, 74
Chaplin, Charlie, 143
Chase, Chevy, 213–214
Churchill, Winston, 39
Cinderella parody, 201
Class, real, 40
Cohen, Myron, 62
Colonna, Jerry, 218
Come Blow Your Horn, 120
Comedy: apropos, 101; black, 204; clubs, 86–87; physical, 213; relief, 103; see Humor
Comparisons, in jokes, 137
Conclusion, wrong, 16
Conway, Tim, 187, 194–195
Coolidge, Calvin, 145
Cosby, Bill, 45, 62, 64
Costello, Lou, 180
Coward, Noel, 17
Crosby, Bing, 66–67, 175
Crystal, Billy, 103

Davis, Sammy, 85–86, 141
De La Bruyere, Jean, 163
Deery, John, 95–96
Defense mechanism, humor as, 31
DeVries, Peter, 114
Dialects, 89
Difference between right word and almost right word, 110; written and spoken stories, 150–151
Dignity, 39–40, 211–214
Diller, Phyllis, 26, 54, 63, 68, 73, 74, 77, 78, 100, 120, 142–143, 219
Distraction, humor as, 77–78
Divisive humor, 211–212
Double entendres, 200
Durante, Jimmy, 166

Earthquake, 23, 99
Embarrassing audience, 214–216
Endings, 108

Ethics, 41–42, 119–120
Ethnic jokes, 41, 182
Exercises, 124–125, 159–169
Experiments, 124–125

Failings of speaker, 75–76
Family history, 111–112
Fear of humor, 46–49, 84
Feldman, Marty, 74
Fields, W.C., 66
Finishes, 108
Flight attendant, 13–14, 35–36
Flop-sweat, 84
Ford, Gerald, 78, 145, 207
Friars, 206

Gallagher, 119, 213
Gephardt, Richard, 102
Gilbert, Brad, 74
Gleason, Jackie, 74
Graves, David, 5
Guidelines for insult humor, 206

Hackett, Buddy, 74
Hardy, Oliver, 74, 143
Heisman, John, 33
Hemingway, Ernest, 122
Herbert, A.P., 81, 120
High Noon, 96
Hill, Napoleon, 217
Hope, Bob, 24, 39, 42, 45, 57–58,
    62–63, 66–68, 74, 76, 78, 85,
    99–100, 115, 127, 128, 131, 136,
    137, 143, 144, 145, 147, 186, 194,
    196, 206, 212, 218
Hughes, Langston, 163
Humility, 94
Humor: aggressive, 210–211
    as aid in clarification, 24, 104–105
    as aid to memory, 25–29, 106
    as attention-getter, 21–23, 103–104
    as attitude, 17, 62–63, 145–146,
        217–219
    as defense mechanism, 31
    as distraction, 77–78
    as means of gaining respect, 19–21, 41,
        94, 194
    as means of relieving tension, 30
    as motivator, 33–34
    as reward, 23, 96–97, 106–107
    dangerous subjects for, 204
    divisive, 211–212
    embarrassing, 214–216
    fear of, 46–49, 84
    harmful forms of, 40–41
    insult, 40–41, 205, 216
    logic in, 54–57; economic, 180–181
    malice in, 41, 46, 199–207
    misinterpretation of, 200–203

physical, 213
pitfalls, 209–216
positioning, 102–107
rehearsing, 49, 92, 177
re-writing, 48, 152–157
sense of, 36–40, 54–60, 163, 219
surprise as element in, 143–144,
    179–180
to defuse attack, 30–32
to reinforce point, 106; exercise, 165
truth in, 37, 59, 142–145, 218
types of, 62–63
understanding, 88

Impersonations, 176
Inattention, 22
Insult humor, 40–41, 205–206

Jillian, Ann, 100
Jim Nabors Hour, 120
Johnny Carson show, 140
Joke services, 117
Joke books, 110–111, 116
Jokes: adapting, 149–157; bizarre, 155,
    207; off-color, 213; telling, 61–62,
    89–90, 175–182
Judgment, 59–60, 94

Kean, Edmund, 44
Kennedy, John F., 125
Kidding yourself, 76–77
King, Alan, 74
King, Martin Luther, 142
Korman, Harvey, 63, 195

Lamb, Charles, 163
Language, 66–67
Laugh-In, 112
Laurel, Stan, 74, 143
Lemmon, Jack, 183
Length of story, 181
Leno, Jay, 145
Levitt, Mortimer, 40
Lewis, Jerry, 73
Lichtenberg, C.C., 163
Lincoln, Abraham, 15, 24, 39, 69,
    104–105, 124
Logic, humor and, 54–55
Los Angeles Times, 118

McArthur, Peter, 163
McCalls, 118
McKay, John, 34
Magic of Believing, 217
Malapropisms, 114–115
Malice, 41, 46, 199–207
Marceau, Marcel, 62
Marquis, Don, 117
Martin, Dean, 76, 141, 189, 206

Marx, Groucho, 145–146
Mary Tyler Moore Show, 103
M*A*S*H, 21
Mason, Jackie, 74, 146
Matthau, Walter, 183
Meader, Vaughan, 64, 65
Medical treatment, 53, 55, 59
Meetings, 169
Memory, exercise, 161–162; humor as aid
    to, 25; tricks, 26–29
Mencken, H.L., 11
Message: 202; making material fit your,
    122–123
Mike Douglas Show, 73
Misinterpretation, 200–203
Mnemonic trick, 26–28
Mnemonics, 96
Mondale, Walter, 16, 24
Murphey, Bob, 61

Nabors, Jim, 134–135
Negative approach, 44–45, 192
Newhart, Bob, 73, 129
Newman, Paul, 214
Number recall, 26–28

Odd Couple, 74, 183
Off-color stories, 182
Offensive humor, 197–207
Old Man and the Sea, 122
Opening jokes, 99–102; exercise,
    164–165
Organizing your material, 120, 160

Parton, Dolly, 78, 203
Peaks and valleys, 186
Peale, Norman Vincent, 217
Pep talk, 25
Performing, 173–184
Persona, speaking, 68–79
Personalizing jokes, 152–157
Phoniness, 87
Photographs, captions for, 168
Picker, David, 162
Pictures, humor creating, 26
Plagiarism, 119–120
Playboy, 118
Politics, 130
Positioning of humor, 102–107
Power of Positive Thinking, 217
Preambles, 184; exercise, 166–167
Professionalism, 100–101
Public domain material, 115–116
Punchline: as surprise, 90, 143–144;
    focused, 130–131;
    hiding the, 143–144;
    how to write, exercises, 167–168;
    paying for, 181;

remembering the, 115, 120
understanding the, 179–180

Queen Elizabeth, 186
Quotations, books of, 117; exercise, 163

Randall, Tony, 189
Reader's Digest, 118
Reagan, Ronald, 16, 31, 99, 141, 203
Rehearsal, 49, 92, 177
Reinforcing your message, 106; exercise,
    165
Remedy for fear of humor, 48
Research, 87, 109–120; exercises, 160,
    162–163
Respect, humor as way of gaining, 21, 41,
    94, 194
Reynolds, Burt, 203
Re-writing stories, 48
Rickles, Don, 40, 45
Rivers, Joan, 68
Roast, 206
Rockne, Knute, 33–34, 100
Rogers, Will, 25, 39, 41, 60, 136,
    145–146, 162, 199–200
Rooney, Mickey, 74
Russell, Bertrand, 117
Russell, Mark, 130
Russell, Mrs. R.R., 200

Sahl, Mort, 134–135, 136–137
Sanders, Col., 87
Sarcasm, 41
Satirist, definition of, 163
Savers, 194–195
See, recognize, accept, 55
Self-image, 38, 76
Sense of humor, 36–40, 163, 189–190;
    losing, 54–60
Setup, 180; exercise, 166–167
Shakespeare, William, 83, 148
Shaw, George Bernard, 162
Shtick, 40
Simon, Neil, 121
Sinatra, Frank, 94
Skelton, Red, 124, 148
Slapstick, 40, 212–213
Smothers Brothers, 141
Soap, 103
Star Search, 74
Stengel, Casey, 106, 118
Style, developing, 64–69, 74–79, 86–87,
    129–131, 151
Surprise in humor, 90, 143–144,
    179–180
"Switching" stories, 132–134

Tahoe, Lake, 51
Tension, 30, 199

Think and Grow Rich, 217
Three, square root of, memory trick, 29
Three Stooges, 212
Three's Company, 22
Timing, 96, 180
Tips on delivering humor, 175–184
Toastmasters International, 72
Tonight Show, 145
Triggering laughs, 179
Truman, Harry S, 136–137
Truth, in humor, 37, 142
Twain, Mark, 110

Uecker, Bob, 74
Ukulele, 25
Understanding material, 69, 88
USS Guam, 20

Verbal photographs, 140
Vietnam troops, 24

Webb, Spud, 118
White, Slappy, 112, 142
Wilde, Oscar, 163, 171
Williams, Robin, 45, 47, 63, 64, 175
Wilson, Flip, 62, 181
Winters, Jonathan, 45, 47
Wooden, John, 194
Word patterns, 145, 146
Writing your own material, 127–134;
    exercises, 159–169; process,
    135–141

Youngman, Henny, 151–152